BOTTLE BY BOTTLE
TO A CLASSIC
COCKTAIL BAR

BOTTLE BY BOTTLE TO A CLASSIC COCKTAIL BAR

Charles of the Ritz and

Carlos of Raffles

Contributing Editor
Sue Parkin

foulsham

London · New York · Toronto · Sydney

foulsham

The Publishing House, Bennetts Close,
Cippenham, Berkshire, SL1 5AP, England

Acknowledgements
Photographs: Mike O'Neill
Props for photographs: The Cocktail Shop,
30 Neal Street, London
and Le Pot, King Edward Court, Windsor

ISBN 0-572-02305-7

Copyright © 1997 W. Foulsham & Co. Ltd.

Originally published as *The Cocktail Year*.

Typeset by ABM Typographics Ltd, Hull
Printed in Hong Kong

Introduction

Bottle By Bottle To A Classic Cocktail Bar contains 365 cocktails, one for every day of the year. There are mouthwatering cocktails for all occasions: romantic cocktails to lure your lover on Valentine's Day, cool blue cocktails to sip by the pool on long summer days and warming punches for winter parties. Each cocktail is illustrated in full colour to give you an idea of what it looks like, which glass to serve it in and how to garnish it.

You can use *Bottle By Bottle To A Classic Cocktail Bar* as a cocktail maker's diary. Space has been left for you to write in your own comments on your cocktail-making extravaganzas, your friends' birthdays, and to remind yourself of other occasions worth celebrating with a seasonal cocktail. Mark your own special occasions by making the cocktail for that day.

The book assumes that your drinks cupboard is empty at the start of the year. You can then start adding drinks, one by one (46 drinks are added in total, at approximately weekly intervals) and at each stage have a large selection of cocktails to choose from. Gradually a good stock of drinks will be accumulated and the more complex cocktail ideas are then suggested. Any cocktail given on a specific date will only contain the drinks that have been introduced by that date.

Preparing cocktails is simplified if ingredients, basic equipment and glasses are stored together. The location will obviously depend on space available: kitchen cupboards, a cocktail cabinet or shelves in a living room. Since it's fun to prepare cocktails in the presence of your guests a trolley may be thought of as an excellent choice and would be a real conversation piece at the start of any occasion.

Your cocktail shopping list

Buying drinks gradually throughout the year will give you an ever-increasing range of cocktail possibilities.

Gin	January 1st	**Port**	June 7th
Italian Vermouth	January 8th	**Plymouth Gin**	June 17th
Dubonnet	January 15th	**Tequila**	June 24th
French Vermouth	January 22nd	**Crème de Banane**	July 1st
Scotch Whisky	January 29th	**Applejack Brandy**	July 8th
Pernod	February 5th	**Maraschino**	July 22nd
Brandy	February 12th	**Yellow Chartreuse**	July 26th
Cointreau	February 19th	**Kummel**	August 5th
Green Crème de Menthe	February 26th	**Amer Picon**	August 19th
Dry Sherry	March 4th	**Bénédictine**	August 26th
Green Chartreuse	March 11th	**Sloe Gin**	September 2nd
Canadian Club Whisky	March 18th	**Fernet Branca**	September 9th
White Rum	March 25th	**Drambuie**	September 16th
Vodka	April 1st	**Irish Whisky**	September 23rd
Campari	April 8th	**Dark and Golden Rum**	September 30th
Blue Curaçao	April 15th	**Kahlua**	October 7th
Galliano	April 22nd	**Grand Marnier**	October 21st
Apricot Brandy	April 29th	**Amaretto di Saronno**	November 1st
Cherry Brandy	May 6th	**White Créme de Menthe**	November 12th
Swedish Punch	May 13th	**Lillet**	November 19th
Calvados	May 20th	**Crème de Cacao**	November 26th
Orange or Brown Curaçao	May 27th	**Tia Maria**	December 3rd
Crème de Cassis	June 3rd	**Kirsch**	December 10th

About the cocktails

How to find the cocktail you want to make

1. If you know the name of the cocktail, there is an alphabetical index on page 118.
2. If you want a cocktail for a particular occasion, look it up under the date.
3. If you want a particular kind of cocktail e.g. a party cocktail, a non-alcoholic cocktail, an after-dinner cocktail or a nourishing night-cap look at the lists on page 117 where you will find suggestions.
4. If you want a cheaper cocktail with fewer ingredients, look at the cocktails at the beginning of the book.
5. If you only have a couple of bottles in you drinks cabinet look at the *Ingredients Guide* on page 114 which will tell you which cocktails you can make with them.

Follow this book and you're going to have a great year!

The basic equipment needed

1. A shaker. This looks something like a miniature Thermos flask, and consists simply of two nickel containers that fit into each other.
2. A mixing glass. This is simply a large tumbler or bar glass.
3. A mixing spoon. This is a spoon holding about the same amount as a teaspoon, but with a long thin handle.
4. A strainer.
5. A lemon squeezer.
6. A muddler. This is an implement used for crushing sugar or bruising fruit, mint, etc.
7. A millilitre measuring glass or a gill measure graded with various fractional parts.

The above are the essentials. Of the other forms of equipment, many are part of the normal culinary equipment. Obviously a corkscrew and bottle opener are required, and for certain recipes a nutmeg grater will be needed. A fruit knife and a fork and spoon for handling fruit will be wanted, too, and there should be an ice pick and a scoop or tongs for handling ice. Finally, straws are needed for the longer drinks, and a bundle of cherry sticks to allow simple manipulation of the cherries, olives, etc., that are served in certain cocktails.

Decanter bottles with stoppers are desirable for ingredients that have to be served in the small measurements known as dashes.

A few cocktails are best made in an electric blender.

Glasses

The photographs and recipes will give you a good guide to the ideal glass to use, but here is a list of the glasses available for serving drinks. Measurements are given as measures, and each measure is equal to 25 ml or 1 gill.

1. Cocktail glasses. Each holds about 75 ml.
2. Small wineglasses or crusta glasses. Each holds about 110 ml.
3. Wineglasses. Each holds about 150 ml.
4. Tumblers or highball glasses. Each holds about $1/2$ pint, or 300 ml.
5. Sherbet glasses are like small tumblers.
6. Liqueur glasses. Each holds about 140 ml. However, fine liqueurs are generally served in large 'balloon' glasses. For ordinary purposes a half-filled cocktail glass is suitable for the serving of liqueur.
7. Pousse café glasses. Also known as *petites flutes*. Each holds about 3 tbsp.
8. Hot drinks glasses vary in size but have handles.

* Remember 1 measure = 1 gill = 25 ml.

Mixers and garnishes

Although you are building up a drinks cabinet with drinks that will keep, you will need to buy mixers as you need them. Once opened they will not keep, so are not included in the overall plan for accumulating drinks.

The following are used as mixers in this book: ginger ale, milk, soda water, ale, wine, sparkling wine, cider and champagne.

Often it is the garnish that makes the cocktail look spectacular. The photographs and recipes will give you ideas for garnishing your cocktails, but look around the cocktail shops or departments of the big stores for other ideas.

Non-alcoholic extras

The spirits and liqueurs will be accumlated over a number of months, but there are a few extra ingredients which will be required. Many may already be in your store cupboard.

The following ingredients are used on one occasion at least, during the year. The fresh ingredients should be purchased as you need them. The bitters and syrups will keep almost indefinitely, so buy and store them with your spirits.

1. Bitters: Angostura, orange, Secrestat, peach.
2. Fruit: lime, lemon, orange, pineapple, cherries (fresh and maraschino) tangerine, apple.
3. Syrups and juices: orange juice, lime cordial, grape juice, pineapple juice, lemon squash, gooseberry syrup, sirop de citron, vanilla syrup, ginger syrup, cherry syrup, orgeat syrup, fraisette (strawberry syrup), maple syrup, grenadine syrup, grapefruit juice.
4. Sugar in lump, powder or syrup form.
5. Eggs.
6. Fresh double cream (sometimes sweetened with a little sugar syrup).
7. Coconut cream.
8. Miscellaneous: blackcurrant jelly, anisette, Worcestershite sauce, tomato ketchup, lemon water, ice, rock candy, pickled onion, olive.

It is worth having the following most common extras to hand when mixing cocktails. Angostura and orange bitters, grenadine

Eight simple rules to cocktail making

1. Do follow the recipe, measure the ingredients and work methodically so that you're in no doubt as to the ingredients you have or have not yet added to the shaker or mixing glass. Unless otherwise stated, each cocktail recipe provides a single drink.
2. Use bitters and syrups with care, a slight error may spoil the drink.
3. A *dash* is equivalent to $\frac{1}{3}$ of a teaspoon (2 ml). Approximately 50 dashes to the measure.
4. **Shaken cocktails**. Place some ice in the shaker, either cracked or cubes and add the ingredients. Replace the upper part of the shaker and holding it with both hands (one being held over the upper part to prevent accidents and spillage) shake briskly to mix and cool ingredients. Too much shaking will melt the ice and dilute the drink. Strain into the glass. *Do not shake* sparkling drinks e.g. champagne, soda water etc.
5. **Stirred or mixed cocktails**. The ingredients are placed in a mixing glass with ice then stirred with a mixing spoon, briskly (unless otherwise stated) until the ingredients are mixed and cooled. Strain into the glass.
6. **Blended cocktails**. Blend the ingredients with the specified amount of crushed ice for a few seconds (not longer or the cocktail will be too diluted). Pour into the glass.
7. **Ice**. Always keep a good supply in the freezer or ice compartment in the refrigerator. There are ice making appliances on the market, which must be the ideal for the serious cocktail maker.
8. Lemon peel is often required to be squeezed on top of the drink. For this, a thin piece of peel should be taken between the fingers and gently squeezed or twisted, so that the juice drops into the drink. The lemon peel should never be put in the glass unless the recipe says so.

January

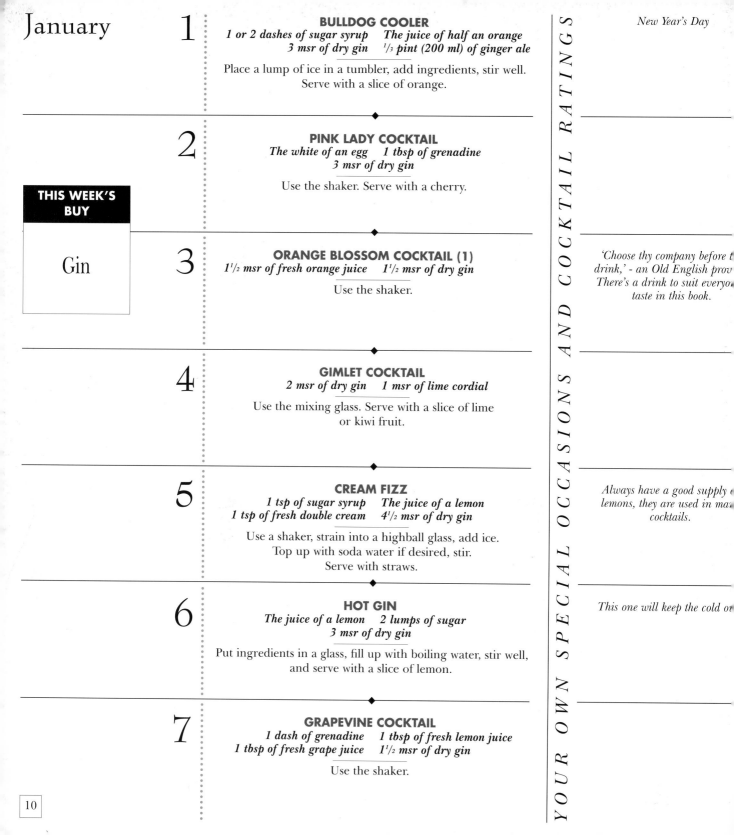

1

BULLDOG COOLER

1 or 2 dashes of sugar syrup   The juice of half an orange
3 msr of dry gin   ¹/₃ pint (200 ml) of ginger ale

Place a lump of ice in a tumbler, add ingredients, stir well.
Serve with a slice of orange.

2

PINK LADY COCKTAIL

The white of an egg   1 tbsp of grenadine
3 msr of dry gin

Use the shaker. Serve with a cherry.

THIS WEEK'S BUY

Gin

3

ORANGE BLOSSOM COCKTAIL (1)

1¹/₂ msr of fresh orange juice   1¹/₂ msr of dry gin

Use the shaker.

4

GIMLET COCKTAIL

2 msr of dry gin   1 msr of lime cordial

Use the mixing glass. Serve with a slice of lime
or kiwi fruit.

5

CREAM FIZZ

1 tsp of sugar syrup   The juice of a lemon
1 tsp of fresh double cream   4¹/₂ msr of dry gin

Use a shaker, strain into a highball glass, add ice.
Top up with soda water if desired, stir.
Serve with straws.

6

HOT GIN

The juice of a lemon   2 lumps of sugar
3 msr of dry gin

Put ingredients in a glass, fill up with boiling water, stir well,
and serve with a slice of lemon.

7

GRAPEVINE COCKTAIL

1 dash of grenadine   1 tbsp of fresh lemon juice
1 tbsp of fresh grape juice   1¹/₂ msr of dry gin

Use the shaker.

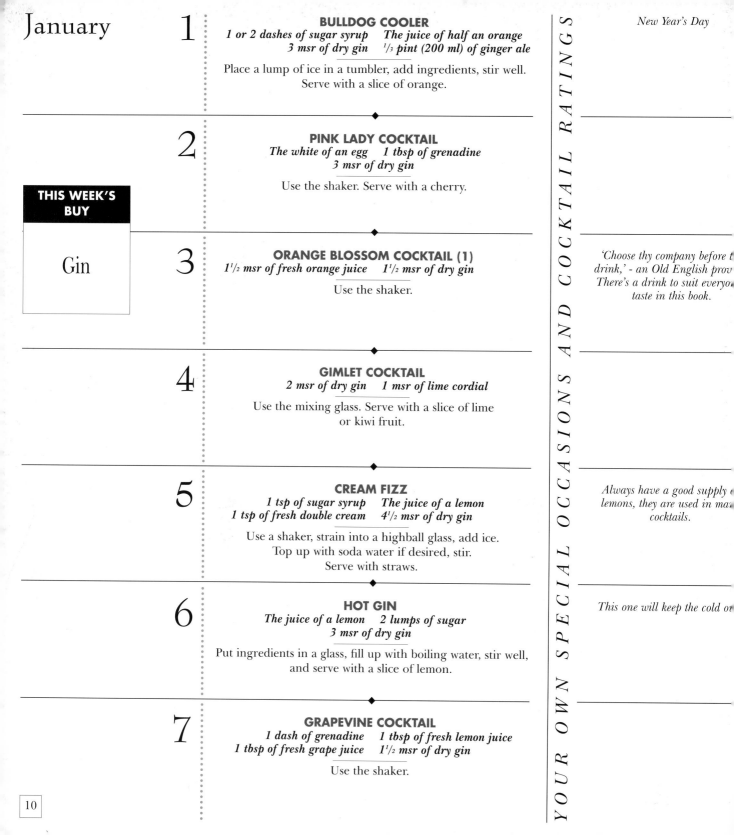

New Year's Day

*'Choose thy company before t[...]
drink,' - an Old English prov[...]
There's a drink to suit everyo[...]
taste in this book.*

*Always have a good supply [...]
lemons, they are used in ma[...]
cocktails.*

This one will keep the cold o[...]

YOUR OWN SPECIAL OCCASIONS AND COCKTAIL RATINGS

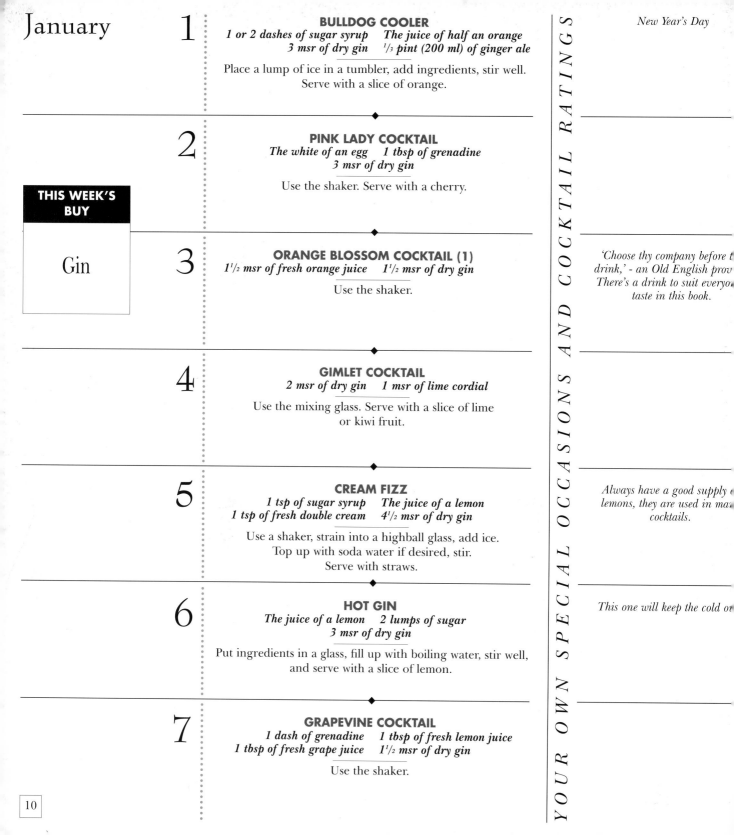

From left: Hot Gin, Gimlet, Bulldog Cooler, Pink Lady Cocktail, Orange Blossom Cocktail (1), Grape Vine Cocktail, Cream Fizz.

January

8

MARTINI COCKTAIL (sweet)
1 msr of Italian vermouth   2 msr of dry gin

Use the mixing glass. Serve with a little lemon-peel juice squeezed on top.

Italian is the sweet vermouth. As it is basically a wine, it will deteriorate once opened and should be drunk within a month, which shouldn't be difficult.

9

CLUB COOLER
1 dash of lemon juice   1 msr of grenadine
2 msr of Italian vermouth   ½ pint (300ml) of soda water

Place a lump of ice in a tumbler. Add the ingredients, stir well. Squeeze a little lemon juice on top, and serve with straws.

THIS WEEK'S BUY

Italian Vermouth

10

RAYMOND HITCH COCKTAIL
The juice of half an orange   1 dash of orange bitters
1 slice of pineapple, to serve   3 msr of Italian vermouth

Use the shaker.

11

PINK ROSE COCKTAIL
1 tsp of grenadine   The white of an egg
1 tsp of fresh lemon juice   3 msr of dry gin
1 tsp of double cream sweetened with a little sugar syrup

Use the shaker. Serve with a cherry.

12

BENNETT COCKTAIL
2 dashes of Angostura bitters   2 msr of dry gin
1 msr of lime juice

Use the shaker. Serve with a slice of lime.

13

CLOVER CLUB COCKTAIL
The juice of a fresh lime (or half a lemon)
The white of an egg   1 msr of grenadine
2 msr of dry gin

Use the shaker.

14

VELOCITY COCKTAIL
2 msr of Italian vermouth   1 msr of dry gin

Use the shaker. Serve with a slice of orange.

From left: Martini Cocktail (sweet), Clover Club Cocktail, Bennett Cocktail, Velocity Cocktail, Raymond Hitch Cocktail, Pink Rose Cocktail, Club Cooler.

January

15

DUBONNET COCKTAIL
$1^1/_2$ msr of Dubonnet $1^1/_2$ msr of dry gin

Use the mixing glass. Serve with a little lemon-peel juice squeezed on top.

Dubonnet is a French aromatic wine.

16

CAFÉ ROYAL APPETISER COCKTAIL
The juice of half an orange $1^1/_2$ msr of Dubonnet
$1^1/_2$ msr of dry gin

Use the shaker. Serve with a slice of orange.

THIS WEEK'S BUY

Dubonnet

17

GIN SLING
$4^1/_2$ msr of dry gin   Sugar syrup according to taste

Put the ingredients in a tumbler containing a lump of ice. Fill up with water or soda water as desired.

18

ALFONSO COCKTAIL
1 lump of sugar   2 dashes of Secrestat bitters
3 msr of Dubonnet   3 msr of champagne

Put the sugar in a wine glass and add the Secrestat bitters. Add one lump of ice and the Dubonnet and stir gently. Fill up with champagne, and top with lemon-peel juice.

19

ANGOSTURA FIZZ
1 tbsp of sugar syrup $1^1/_2$ msr of Angostura bitters
3 msr of lemon juice   The white of an egg

Use a shaker, strain into a highball glass, add ice. Top up with soda water, if desired. Stir. Serve with straws.

Angostura is named after the town in Venezuela, where the aromatic bitters were first made in 1824. The same recipe is still used, though Angostura bitters are now produced in Trinidad.

20

ROYAL COCKTAIL
1 dash of Angostura bitters   1 dash of orange bitters
1 msr of Dubonnet   2 msr of dry gin

Use the mixing glass. Serve with a cherry and a little lemon-peel juice squeezed on top.

21

CIDER COCKTAIL
1 dash of Angostura bitters $4^1/_2$ gill of cider
$^1/_2$ tsp of sugar syrup

Use the mixing glass, half filled with broken ice. Stir well. Strain into a glass. Serve with a slice of lemon on top. Non-alcoholic cider may be used.

YOUR OWN SPECIAL OCCASIONS AND COCKTAIL RATINGS

Clockwise from left: Cider Cocktail, Alfonso Cocktail, Dubonnet Cocktail, Angostura Fizz, Gin Sling, Café Royal Appetiser Cocktail, Royal Cocktail (centre).

January

22

MARTINI COCKTAIL (dry)

1 dash of orange bitters   *2 msr of dry gin*
1 msr of Martini vermouth (dry)

Use the mixing glass. Serve with a little lemon-peel juice squeezed on top and a slice of lemon.

23

QUEEN'S COCKTAIL

1 slice of crushed pineapple   *1 tbsp of French vermouth*
1 tbsp of Italian vermouth   *1½ msr of dry gin*

Use the mixing glass. Decorate with a small piece of pineapple.

24

R.A.C. COCKTAIL

1 dash of orange bitters   *1 dash of grenadine*
1 tbsp of French vermouth   *1 tbsp of Italian vermouth*
1½ msr of dry gin

Using the mixing glass. Serve with a cherry and a little orange-peel juice squeezed on top.

25

YELLOW RATTLER COCKTAIL

1 tbsp of fresh orange juice   *1 tbsp of French vermouth*
1 tbsp of Italian vermouth   *1 tbsp of dry gin*

Use the shaker. Serve with a small crushed pickled onion.

26

POLO COCKTAIL

The juice of half a lime or quarter of a lemon
2 msr of French vermouth   *1 msr of Italian vermouth*
2 msr of dry gin

Use the shaker. Serve with a slice of lemon.

27

ORANGE BLOSSOM COCKTAIL (2)

1 dash of orange bitters   *1 dash of grenadine*
1½ msr of orange juice   *1½ msr of dry gin*

Use the shaker. Serve with a small slice of orange.

28

ROYAL FIZZ

1 tsp of sugar syrup or grenadine
The juice of 1 lemon   *1 egg*
4½ msr of dry gin

Use a shaker. Strain into a highball glass, add ice. Top up with soda water. Serve with straws.

YOUR OWN SPECIAL OCCASIONS AND COCKTAIL RATINGS

An all-time classic.

French *as it has always been called, is the dry aromatized wine. It deteriorates once opened, so it is suggested that it should be drunk within two weeks of opening.*

A fizz is always shaken, which gives the drink a good consistency.

From left: Martini Cocktail (dry), Queen's Cocktail, R.A.C. Cocktail, Royal Fizz, Yellow Rattler Cocktail, Polo Cocktail, Orange Blossom Cocktail (2).

January

29

THISTLE COCKTAIL
2 dashes of Angostura bitters   1½ msr of Italian vermouth
1½ msr of Scotch whisky

Use the mixing glass.

30

SCOTCH MIST COCKTAIL
2 msr of Scotch whisky   cracked ice
twist of lemon peel

Use old-fashioned glasses. Shake Scotch whisky with cracked ice and pour unstrained. Add twist of lemon peel. Serve with straws.

31

WHISKY TODDY
1 tsp of sugar   4½ msr of Scotch whisky

Dissolve the sugar in hot water, and add the whisky. Fill up with boiling water. Serve with a slice of lemon on top.

February

1

GAELIC COFFEE
Hot coffee   2 tsp of sugar
2 msr of Scotch whisky   fresh double cream

Pour coffee into a glass, stir in sugar and whisky. Pour the cream very gently over the back of a warmed spoon.
DO NOT STIR.

2

AFFINITY COCKTAIL
2 dashes of Angostura bitters   1 msr of French vermouth
1 msr of Italian vermouth   1 msr of Scotch whisky

Use the mixing glass. Serve with a cherry and a little lemon-peel juice squeezed on top.

3

WEMBLEY COCKTAIL
1 msr of fresh pineapple juice   1 msr of French vermouth
1 msr of Scotch whisky

Use the shaker.

4

WHISKY COOLER
2 dashes of orange bitters   3 msr of Scotch whisky
½ pint (300 ml) soda water

Place a lump of ice in a tumbler, add ingredients, stir well, and serve with a slice of orange. If you want to make it sweeter, include one or two dashes of sugar syrup.

Spending a day outside or in [the] country? Make up a flask of t[his] toddy to keep you warm.

YOUR OWN SPECIAL OCCASIONS AND COCKTAIL RATINGS

18

Clockwise from left: Affinity Cocktail, Thistle Cocktail, Scotch Mist Cocktail, Wembley Cocktail, Whisky Cooler, Gaelic Coffee, Whisky Toddy.

19

February

5
APPETISER COCKTAIL
1 dash of Pernod   1½ msr of Dubonnet
1½ msr of dry gin

Use the shaker. Serve with a little lemon-peel juice squeezed on top.

6
DUCHESS COCKTAIL
1 msr of Italian vermouth   1 msr of Pernod
1 msr of French (or dry Martini) vermouth

Use the mixing glass.

7
WHIZ-BANG COCKTAIL
2 dashes of Pernod   2 dashes of grenadine
2 dashes of orange bitters   1 msr of French vermouth
2 msr of Scotch whisky

Use the mixing glass. Serve with a slice of orange.

THIS WEEK'S BUY

Pernod

8
NICK'S OWN COCKTAIL
1 dash of Angostura bitters   1 dash of Pernod
1½ msr of Italian vermouth

Use the mixing glass. Serve with a cherry and a little lemon-peel juice squeezed on top.

9
BELMONT COCKTAIL
1 tsp of sweet cream   1 msr of grenadine
2 msr of dry gin

Use the shaker.

10
TIGER'S TAIL COCKTAIL
2 msr of Pernod   4 msr of orange juice
A slice of orange

Serve over ice. Use old fashioned glass (a small tumbler).

11
WHITE-HORSE DAISY
2 dashes of grenadine   3 msr of lemon juice
1 tsp of Pernod   The white of an egg
3 msr of White Horse whisky

Shake well, and strain. Serve in an ice-filled tumbler. Top up with soda water. Stir and decorate with fruit.

YOUR OWN SPECIAL OCCASIONS AND COCKTAIL RATINGS

Pernod is a popular aniseed flavoured aperitif. In France the French drink it well-chilled, mixed with water. It is also a good addition to many cocktails.

The flavour may be improved if a dash of anisette is added.

From left: Nick's Own Cocktail, White Horse Daisy, Duchess Cocktail, Whiz-bang Cocktail, Belmont Cocktail, Appetiser Cocktail, Tiger's Tail Cocktail.

February 12

PRESTO COCKTAIL

For four persons:
4 dashes of Pernod   2 msr of fresh orange juice
2 msr of Italian vermouth   8 msr of brandy

Use the mixing glass. Serve with a slice of orange.

13

PLAIN EGG NOGG

1 egg   1 tsp of sugar syrup
4½ msr of brandy or rum   4½ msr of milk

Prepare in a shaker, half-filled with broken ice. Strain into a glass. Sprinkle with grated nutmeg. Stir in more milk if desired.

14

VALENTINE'S CHAMPAGNE COCKTAIL

1 lump of sugar   2 dashes of Angostura bitters
2 pieces of lemon peel   Champagne

Put a lump of sugar in a glass, add the Angostura bitters. Squeeze the juice of one piece of lemon-peel into the glass. Add an ice cube, fill with champagne. Stir gently, squeeze the juice of the other piece of lemon-peel on top.

15

WASHINGTON COCKTAIL

2 dashes of Angostura bitters   2 dashes of sugar syrup
1 msr of brandy   2 msr of French vermouth

Use the mixing glass.

THIS WEEK'S BUY

Brandy

16

LINSTEAD COCKTAIL

1 dash of Pernod   1½ msr of Scotch whisky
1½ msr of sweetened pineapple juice

Use the shaker. Serve with a little lemon-peel juice squeezed on top.

17

CIDER CUP (1)

1 quart of cider, preferably chilled
1 bottle of soda water, preferably chilled
6 msr of brandy   The juice of a lemon

Pour ingredients over ice into a jug and stir. Decorate with orange. Serve immediately. Serves 4.

18

CHARLES COCKTAIL

1 dash of Angostura bitters   1½ msr of Italian vermouth
1½ msr of brandy

Use the mixing glass.

If a creamier consistency is preferred use cream instead of milk, or a mixture of milk and cream.

St. Valentine's Day.

One bottle of champagne will make six cocktails.

Clockwise from left: Plain Egg Nog, Cider Cup (1), Valentine's Champagne Cocktail, Linstead Cocktail, Washington Cocktail, Presto Cocktail, Charles Cocktail.

19

CLARET CUP
1 bottle of claret, preferably chilled
1 bottle of soda water, preferably chilled
1½ msr of Cointreau   3 msr of brandy
1 tsp of lemon juice

Place a large piece of ice in a glass jug or bowl, add ingredients and stir well. Decorate with fruit. Serve immediately. Serves 4.

◆

20

HULA-HULA COCKTAIL
1 or 2 dashes of Cointreau   1 msr of fresh orange juice
1 msr of dry gin

Use the shaker.

◆

THIS WEEK'S BUY

Cointreau

21

LUIGI COCKTAIL
1 tsp of grenadine   1 dash of Cointreau
The juice of half a tangerine   1½ msr of French vermouth
1½ msr of dry gin

Use the shaker. Serve with a little lemon-peel juice squeezed and served on top.

◆

22

EGG SOUR
1 egg   1½ msr of Cointreau
1½ msr of brandy   3 dashes of lemon juice
Sugar or sugar syrup to taste

Prepare the shaker, half-filled with broken ice. Shake well, and strain into a glass.

◆

23

WYOMING SWING COCKTAIL
The juice of ¼ of an orange   ½ tsp of caster sugar
1½ msr of French vermouth   1½ msr of Italian vermouth

Use the mixing glass. Serve in a wine glass and top with soda water.

◆

24

ROLLS-ROYCE COCKTAIL
1 msr of brandy   1 msr of Cointreau
1 msr of orange juice   Egg white

Use the shaker.

◆

25

MONKEY GLAND COCKTAIL
2 dashes of Pernod   2 dashes of grenadine
1 msr of fresh orange juice   2 msr of dry gin

Use the shaker. Serve with a kumquat (available at this time of year) or a cocktail cherry.

YOUR OWN SPECIAL OCCASIONS AND COCKTAIL RATINGS

Cointreau is very refined, colourless, orange-flavoured liqueur. It is made in the Anjou district of France.

Kumquats are mainly imported from Morocco and are eaten with the skin. If they are plentiful, freeze some for later in the year.

From left: Monkey Gland Cocktail, Egg Sour, Hula-hula Cocktail, Luigi Cocktail, Claret Cup, Wyoming Swing Cocktail, Rolls Royce Cocktail.

26

ALEXANDER'S SISTER COCKTAIL
1 tbsp of crème de menthe   1 tbsp of sweet cream
1½ msr of dry gin

Use the shaker.

Crème de Menthe is a grain spirit, flavoured with peppermint and sweetened. It sold in its natural colourless state or coloured green.

27

ORANGES AND LEMONS COCKTAIL
1 orange   1 lemon
2 or 3 cherries   1 dash of crème de menthe
2 tsp of powdered sugar

Peel the orange and lemon, separate into sections, and place in a sundae glass. Put the cherries in the middle, add the crème de menthe. Serve with powdered sugar on top. To frost the glass: moisten edges of glass with crème de menthe, dip in caster sugar.

THIS WEEK'S BUY

Crème
de
Menthe

28

BRANDY SOUR
1 tsp of sugar syrup   3 msr of brandy
The juice of half a lemon (or equal parts of lemon and lime)

Mix in a shaker, half-filled with broken ice. Strain into a small wine glass or a brandy glass. If desired add a little soda water and decorate with fruit (e.g. lemon or lime slices).

29

GLAD EYE COCKTAIL
1 msr of crème de menthe   2 msr of Pernod

Use the shaker.

Leap Year Day. If there's a 29th this year, make it an occasion to try this drink - it delicious.

March 1

THIRD DEGREE COCKTAIL
4 dashes of Pernod   1 msr of French vermouth
2 msr of dry gin

Use the mixing glass. Serve with an olive.

St. David's Day - patron saint of Wales.

2

JOURNALIST COCKTAIL
2 dashes of fresh lemon juice   2 dashes of Cointreau
1 dash of Angostura bitters   ½ msr of French vermouth
½ msr of Italian vermouth   2 msr of dry gin

Use the shaker. Serve with a slice of orange and lemon.

3

MORNING GLORY FIZZ
½ tsp of sugar syrup   The juice of half a lemon
The white of an egg   2 dashes of Pernod
4½ msr of Scotch whisky

Use a shaker, strain into a highball glass, add ice. Top up with soda water, if desired. Stir. Serve with straws.

Don't let the name put you o[f] making it any time of the da[y] or night.

From left: Morning Glory Fizz, Glad Eye Cocktail, Brandy Sour, Oranges and Lemons Cocktail, Third Degree Cocktail, Journalist Cocktail, Alexander's Sister Cocktail.

4

ROC-A-COE COCKTAIL
1¹/₂ msr of sherry   1¹/₂ msr of dry gin

Use the mixing glass. Serve with a cherry.

5

BRAZIL COCKTAIL
1 dash of Angostura bitters   1 dash of Pernod
1¹/₂ msr of French vermouth   1¹/₂ msr of dry sherry

Use the mixing glass. Serve with a little lemon-peel juice
squeezed on top.

6

ADDINGTON COCKTAIL
1¹/₂ msr of French vermouth   1¹/₂ msr of Italian vermouth

Use the mixing glass. Serve in a wine glass, top with soda,
squeeze a little orange-peel juice and serve on top.

7

ALE POSSET
1 pint (600 ml) of milk   1 cup (8 fl oz) of sherry
1 cup (8 fl oz) of ale   4 lumps of sugar

Heat the milk until it almost boils. Meanwhile mix the
sherry, ale and sugar in a jug, and to this add the hot milk.
Serve with grated nutmeg. Serves 3.

**THIS WEEK'S
BUY**

Dry
Sherry

8

ROB ROY COCKTAIL
1 msr of Scotch whisky   1 msr of sweet vermouth
1 dash of Angostura bitters

Use the mixing glass. Add a cherry.

9

WHIZ-BANG COOLER
3 msr of dry gin   ¹/₂ pint (300 ml) ginger ale

Place a lump of ice in a tumbler, add ingredients, stir well,
and serve with a dash of crème de menthe and a sprig of
mint on top.

10

GRAPEFRUIT AND ORANGEADE
2 grapefruits   6 msr of orange juice
6 msr of cider (or apple juice)   ¹/₄ lb of loaf sugar
Soda water

Rub the loaf sugar on the rind of the grapefruits and
oranges, put into a jug. Pour over strained grapefruit and
orange juice. Stir to dissolve sugar. Just prior to serving add
cider, soda water and ice. Decorate with slices of fruit.

YOUR OWN SPECIAL OCCASIONS AND COCKTAIL RATINGS

A perfect aperitif.

 Clockwise from left: Ale Posset, Roc-a-coe Cocktail, Addington Cocktail, Brazil Cocktail, Grapefruit and Orangeade, Whiz-bang Cooler, Rob Roy Cocktail.

March

11 — ST. GERMAIN COCKTAIL

The juice of ½ a lemon　　*The juice of ¼ of a grapefruit*
The white of an egg　　*3 msr of green Chartreuse*

Use the shaker.

Chartreuse is an ancient herbal liqueur from France. Green or yellow varieties are available, the green is stronger and the yellow is sweeter.

12 — ORANGE FIZZ

1 tsp of sugar syrup　　*The juice of an orange*
4½ msr of dry gin

Use a shaker, strain into a highball glass, add ice. Top up with soda water, stir. Serve with straws and a slice of orange.

13 — MOSELLE COBBLER

3 or 4 dashes of sugar syrup　　*1 or 2 dashes of lemon juice*
4 dashes of brandy　　*6 msr of Moselle*

Make in a shaker, half-filled with broken ice. Strain into a tumbler half-full of broken ice. Serve with a straw.

THIS WEEK'S BUY

Green Chartreuse

14 — CHAMPS ELYSÉES COCKTAIL

1 dash of Angostura bitters　　*1 tbsp of Chartreuse*
1 tbsp of sweetened lemon juice　　*1½ msr of brandy*

Use the shaker.

15 — BRANDY DAISY

1½ msr of grenadine　　*3 msr of lemon juice*
3 msr of lime juice　　*3 msr of brandy*

Shake well, and strain into an ice-filled tumbler. Top up with soda water. Stir and decorate with fruit. Alternative serving: strain into and ice-filled wine glass, omit soda water. Decorate with fruit. Half quantities for this method.

16 — PUSSY FOOT COCKTAIL

2 msr of fresh orange juice　　*2 msr of fresh lemon juice*
2 msr of lime juice　　*1 dash of grenadine*
The yolk of an egg

Use the shaker.

17 — EMERALD COOLER

The juice of half a lemon　　*3 msr of brandy*
1½ msr green crème de menthe　　*6 msr of pineapple juice*

Stir ingredients in a tumbler, add ice. Serve with straws.

St Patrick's Day (Ireland's patron saint).

 Clockwise from top left: Champs Elysées Cocktail, Orange Fizz, Brandy Daisy, Moselle Cobbler, St. Germain Cocktail, Pussy Foot Cocktail, Emerald Cooler.

March

18

NEW YORK COOLER

1½ msr of lemon squash   3 dashes of grenadine
3 msr of Canadian Club whisky   ⅓ pint of soda water

Place a lump of ice in a tumbler, add ingredients. Stir well. Squeeze a little lemon-peel on top and serve with a slice of lemon.

19

ROCK AND RYE COCKTAIL

1 piece of rock candy   The juice of a lemon
3 msr of Canadian Club whisky

Dissolve the rock candy in the whisky, and add the lemon juice.

20

SOUL'S KISS COCKTAIL

2 msr of fresh orange juice   2 msr of Dubonnet
4 msr of French vermouth   4 msr Canadian Club whisky

Use the shaker. Serve with slices of orange. Serves 4.

21

MOUNTAIN COCKTAIL

The white of an egg   ½ msr of fresh lemon juice
½ msr of French vermouth   ½ msr of Italian vermouth
1½ msr of Canadian Club whisky

Use the shaker.

THIS WEEK'S BUY

Canadian Club Whisky

22

LOS ANGELES COCKTAIL

1 dash of Italian vermouth   The juice of a lemon
1 egg   4 tsp of sugar
12 msr of Canadian Club whisky

Use the shaker. Serves 4.

23

BLACK VELVET COCKTAIL

Half-cold Guinness   Half-chilled dry champagne

Serve in ½ pint (300 ml) or 1 pint (600 ml) measures; add Guinness to champagne.

24

CAFÉ DE PARIS COCKTAIL

3 dashes of anisette, or Pernod   The white of an egg
A dash of sugar syrup   1 tsp of fresh cream
3 msr of dry gin

Use the shaker.

YOUR OWN SPECIAL OCCASIONS AND COCKTAIL RATINGS

Canadian whisky was originally made by Scots and Irish settlers in Canada. It is a light-bodied whisky well suited to cocktails and mixing.

Also good drunk at lower altitudes.

Clockwise from left: Soul's Kiss Cocktail, Rock and Rye Cocktail, Café de Paris Cocktail, Black Velvet Cocktail, New York Cooler, Los Angeles Cocktail, Mountain Cocktail.

25
CUBA LIBRE COCKTAIL
The juice of half a lime   2 msr of white rum
The peel of half a lime in one piece
Coca-Cola

Place juice and peel of the lime in a tumbler, add ice, rum and fill up with Coca-Cola. Stir and serve.

26
SPRING SHAKE-UP
3 dashes of grenadine   1 dash of Angostura bitters
1 tbsp of Cointreau   1¹/₂ msr of white rum
4¹/₂ msr of pineapple juice

Shake all ingredients together, strain into a tumbler, add ice. Serve with straws. Decorate with a strawberry and cherry.

27
RUM COOLER
1 tsp of sugar syrup   1¹/₂ msr of lime juice
3 msr of white rum   ¹/₃ pint of soda water

Place a lump of ice in a tumbler, add ingredients, stir well. Serve with a slice of lime.

THIS WEEK'S BUY

White Rum

28
BACARDI CRUSTA
1 tsp of sugar syrup   1 msr of lemon juice
2 dashes of Angostura bitters   1 tsp of Pernod
2 msr of Bacardi rum

Make in a shaker half-filled with broken ice. Place a spiral of lemon rind in a frosted crusta (small wine) glass, add ice and strained cocktail. To frost the glass: moisten edges with lemon juice then dip rim in caster sugar.

29
PIÑA COLADA
4¹/₂ msr white rum   6 msr of pineapple juice
3 msr coconut cream

Blend the ingredients with two scoops of crushed ice. Serve in an ice-filled pineapple shell or large glass. Garnish with fruit and parasols.

30
SCORPION
1 tbsp of brandy   3 msr of white rum
1 tbsp of orange juice   1 tsp of orgeat syrup

Use the shaker. Strain into a bowl-shaped glass, half-filled with crushed ice. Garnish with a fresh flower.

31
CASABLANCA
3 tbsp white rum   3 msr of pineapple juice
1¹/₂ msr of coconut cream   2 dashes of grenadine

Use the shaker. Serve in a large wine glass and garnish with a cherry, a slice of orange and a slice of pineapple.

Bacardi is a brand of white rum, originally from Cuba.

From left: Spring Shake-Up, Cuba Libre Cocktail, Piña Colada, Scorpion, Casablanca, Bacardi Crusta, Rum Cooler.

April

1 — BOO BOO'S SPECIAL

2 msr of orange juice   2 msr of pineapple juice
A little lemon juice   1 dash of Angostura bitters
1 dash of grenadine

Use the shaker. Serve in a tumbler garnished with slices of pineapple and orange.

2 — BLOODY MARY

2 msr of vodka   2 dashes of Worcester sauce
A little lemon juice   Tomato juice

Use a 6 oz (175 ml) goblet. Add ice, vodka, Worcester sauce, a little lemon juice. Top with tomato juice and stir with a stick of celery.

3 — SANDMARTIN COCKTAIL

1 tsp of green Chartreuse   1½ msr of Italian vermouth
1½ msr of dry gin

Use the mixing glass. Serve with a lemon-peel juice squeezed on top.

THIS WEEK'S BUY

Vodka

---

4 — BALALAIKA COCKTAIL

1 msr of vodka   1 msr of Cointreau
1 msr of lemon juice

Use the shaker.

5 — DANDY COCKTAIL

1 dash of Angostura bitters   1 piece of orange peel
3 dashes of Cointreau   1½ msr of Dubonnet
1 piece of lemon peel   1½ msr Canadian Club whisky

Use the shaker.

6 — SCREWDRIVER COCKTAIL

2 msr of vodka   2 msr of orange juice

Serve with ice in a frosted glass. Decorate with a slice of orange. To frost the glass: moisten rim of glass with orange juice, then dip in caster sugar.

7 — VODKATINI COCKTAIL

2 msr of vodka   1 msr of dry vermouth
A twist of lemon peel

Use the mixing glass.

YOUR OWN SPECIAL OCCASIONS AND COCKTAIL RATINGS

Clockwise from left: Dandy Cocktail, Vodkatini Cocktail, Balalaika Cocktail, Sandmartin Cocktail, Boo Boo's Special, Screwdriver Cocktail, Bloody Mary.

April

8 — S.W.1 COCKTAIL
1 msr of vodka   1 msr of Campari
1 msr of orange juice   Egg white

Use the shaker. Serve with cocktail cherries.

9 — BACARDI COCKTAIL
1 msr of fresh lime juice   1 msr of Bacardi rum
Sugar syrup to taste

Use the shaker. Serve with a slice of lime.

10 — AMERICANO COCKTAIL
1 msr of Campari   1 msr of sweet vermouth

Stir and fill with soda. Serve with ice.

THIS WEEK'S BUY

Campari

11 — LADIES' COCKTAIL
2 dashes of Angostura bitters   2 dashes of Pernod
2 dashes of anisette   3 msr Canadian Club Whisky

Use the mixing glass. Serve with a slice of pineapple on top.

12 — NEGRONI COCKTAIL
1 msr of dry gin   1 msr of sweet vermouth
1 msr of Campari

Stir. Serve with ice and half slice of orange.

13 — TROPICAL DAWN
1½ msr of gin   1½ msr of fresh orange juice
1 tbsp of Campari

Half-fill the shaker with crushed ice. Add the gin and orange juice. Shake. Pour into a glass. Pour the Campari over the top. Decorate with a slice of orange and cherries.

14 — FALLEN ANGEL COCKTAIL
1 dash of Angostura bitters   2 dashes of crème de menthe
The juice of half a lemon   3 msr of dry gin

Use the shaker.

Campari is an Italian bitters, dark red in colour. Bitters are a perfect apéritif for stimulating the appetite.

YOUR OWN SPECIAL OCCASIONS AND COCKTAIL RATINGS

From left: *Americano Cocktail, Fallen Angel Cocktail, Bacardi Cocktail, Negroni Cocktail, Ladies' Cocktail, Tropical Dawn, S.W.1 Cocktail.*

April

15
BREAKFAST EGG NOGG
1 egg   1½ msr of blue Curaçao
4½ of brandy   6 msr of milk

Prepare in a shaker, half-filled with broken ice. Strain into a glass, sprinkle with grated nutmeg. Stir in more milk if desired. If you prefer, use cream instead of milk, or mix milk and cream.

16
BLUE BIRD COCKTAIL
4 dashes of Angostura bitters   5 dashes of blue Curaçao
3 msr of dry gin

Use the shaker. Serve with a cherry and a little lemon-peel juice squeezed on top.

17
BOSOM CARESSER COCKTAIL
3 dashes of grenadine   The yolk of an egg
1 msr of blue Curaçao   2 msr of brandy

Use the shaker.

18
TRUE BLUE
3 msr of blue Curaçao   1½ msr of lime juice
Soda water

Serve in a tumbler with a few lumps of ice. Serve with a spiral of lime.

19
MILLIONAIRE COCKTAIL (1)
The white of an egg   2 dashes of blue Curaçao
1 msr of grenadine   2 msr Canadian Club whisky

Use the shaker.

20
BLUE SOUR
3 msr of blue Curaçao   The juice of half a lemon
1 tsp of sugar syrup

Put the ingredients in a shaker, half-filled with broken ice. Shake. Strain into a frosted glass. To frost the glass: moisten rim with the Curaçao, then dip in caster sugar.

21
EAST INDIA COCKTAIL
2 dashes of Angostura bitters   2 dashes of pineapple juice
2 dashes of blue Curaçao   3 msr of brandy

Use the shaker. Serve with a cherry and a little lemon-peel juice squeezed on top.

YOUR OWN SPECIAL OCCASIONS AND COCKTAIL RATINGS

This orange flavoured liqueur may be obtained in several colours - orange, blue, green or white - all identical in taste.

Clockwise from left: Blue Bird Cocktail, Blue Sour, East India Cocktail, True Blue, Millionaire Cocktail, Breakfast Egg Nog, Bosom Caresser Cocktail (centre).

April

22

HARVEY WALLBANGER COCKTAIL
2 msr of vodka   4 msr of orange juice
2 tsp of Galliano

Shake and strain onto ice. Float Galliano on top.
Serve with straws.

23

OLD PAL COCKTAIL
1 msr of French vermouth   1 msr of Campari
1 msr of Canadian Club whisky

Use the mixing glass.

24

GOLDEN DREAM COCKTAIL
2 msr of Galliano   1 tbsp of Cointreau
1 tbsp of orange juice   1 tbsp of fresh double cream

Shake and serve in champagne glass.

THIS WEEK'S BUY

Galliano

25

MANHATTAN COCKTAIL (dry)
2 dashes of Angostura bitters   1½ msr of French vermouth
1½ msr of Canadian Club whisky

Use the mixing glass. Serve with an olive or cherry and little
lemon-peel juice squeezed on top.

26

BACARDI SPECIAL COCKTAIL
1 tsp of grenadine   The juice of half a lime
1 msr of dry gin   2 msr of Bacardi rum

Use the shaker. Serve with a slice of lime.

27

SIDECAR COCKTAIL
1 msr of fresh lemon juice   1 msr of Cointreau
1 msr of brandy

Use the shaker.

28

INK STREET COCKTAIL
1 msr of fresh lemon juice   1 msr of fresh orange juice
1 msr of Canadian Club whisky

Use the shaker. Serve with a slice of orange and lemon.

Galliano was named after a famous nineteenth century Italian major of the same name. It is a herbal liqueur, produced in Milan.

St. George's Day - patron saint of England.

Clockwise from top left: Old Pal Cocktail, Manhattan Cocktail, Golden Dream Cocktail, Harvey Wallbanger Cocktail, Sidecar Cocktail, Ink Street Cocktail, Bacardi Special Cocktail.

April

29

FAIRY BELLE COCKTAIL

1 tsp of grenadine   *The white of an egg*
1 tbsp apricot brandy   *3 tbsp dry gin*

Use the shaker.

30

CUBAN COCKTAIL

1 tbsp of fresh lime juice   *1 tbsp apricot brandy*
$1^{1}/_{2}$ msr of brandy

Using the mixing glass. Serve with a slice of lime.

May

1

CHAMPAGNE COBBLER

3 or 4 dashes of sugar syrup   *1 or 2 dashes of lemon juice*
2 dashes of old brandy   *6 msr of champagne*

Prepare in the mixing glass (*not* the shaker), half-filled with broken ice. Stir gently, and strain into a tumbler half-full of broken ice. Decorate with fruit, and serve with a straw.

2

PARADISE COCKTAIL

1 msr of fresh orange juice   *1 msr of apricot brandy*
1 msr dry gin

Use the shaker. Serve with a slice of orange.

THIS WEEK'S BUY

Apricot Brandy

3

PICCADILLY COCKTAIL

1 dash of Pernod   *1 dash of grenadine*
1 msr of French vermouth   *2 msr of dry gin*

Use the shaker.

4

GIN DAISY

1 tbsp of grenadine   *3 msr of lemon juice*
3 msr of dry gin

Shake well, and strain into an ice-filled tumbler. Top up with soda water. Stir and decorate with fruit. Alternative serving: strain into an ice-filled wine glass onit soda water. Decorate with fruit. Half quantities for this method.

5

FOURTH DEGREE COCKTAIL

4 dashes of Pernod   *1 tbsp of French vermouth*
1 tbsp of Italian vermouth   *$1^{1}/_{2}$ msr of dry gin*

Use the mixing glass. Serve with a cherry.

YOUR OWN SPECIAL OCCASIONS AND COCKTAIL RATINGS

From left: Cuban Cocktail, Fairy Belle Cocktail, Champagne Cobbler, Paradise Cocktail, Piccadilly Cocktail, Fourth Degree Cocktail, Gin Daisy.

May

6
SINGAPORE SLING
1 msr of lemon juice   2 msr of gin
1 msr of cherry brandy

Put the ingredients in a shaker, half-filled with broken ice. Shake well, and strain into an ice-filled tumbler. Fill up with soda water and stir. Serve with fruit and a parasol.

7
BRANDY FIX
1 tsp of sugar syrup   The juice of half a lemon
1½ msr of brandy   1½ msr of cherry brandy
A little water to taste

Place ingredients in a tumbler, stir. Fill up glass with crushed ice. Decorate with fruit and serve with straws.

8
BRANDY SMASH
½ lump of sugar   4 sprigs of fresh mint
3 msr of brandy

In the shaker dissolve the sugar in a little water. Quickly stir in the mint and remove. Half-fill the shaker with ice, add brandy, shake well, then strain. Serve in a wine glass decorated with fruit.

9
BLOOD AND SAND COCKTAIL
1 tbsp of fresh orange juice   1 tbsp of Italian vermouth
1 tbsp of cherry brandy   1 tbsp of Scotch whisky

Use the mixing glass. Serve with a slice of orange and a cherry.

10
LONDON COCKTAIL
2 dashes of orange bitters   2 dashes of sugar syrup
2 dashes of Pernod   3 msr of dry gin

Use the mixing glass. Serve with olives and a little lemon-peel juice squeezed on top.

11
VANDERBILT COCKTAIL
2 dashes of Angostura bitters   3 dashes of sugar syrup
1 tbsp of cherry brandy   1 tbsp of brandy

Use the mixing glass.

12
COOPERSTOWN COCKTAIL
1 msr of French vermouth   1 msr of Italian vermouth
1 msr of dry gin   2 sprigs of fresh mint

Use the mixing glass. Serve with a cherry on top.

YOUR OWN SPECIAL OCCASIONS AND COCKTAIL RATINGS

This drink originated from Raffles Hotel in Singapore.

 Top from left: Blood and Sand Cocktail, Brandy Fix, Singapore Sling, Brandy Smash. Bottom from left: Cooperstown Cocktail, London Cocktail, Vanderbilt Cocktail.

May

13

WALDORF COCKTAIL
1 msr of dry gin   2 msr of Swedish punch
The juice of half a lime or a quarter of a lemon

Use the mixing glass.

14

DOCTOR COCKTAIL
2 msr of Swedish punch
1 msr of fresh lime juice (or lemon juice)

Use the shaker.

15

BOOMERANG COCKTAIL
1 dash of Angostura bitters   1 msr of Swedish punch
1 dash of fresh lemon juice   1 msr Canadian Club whisky
1 msr French (or dry Martini) vermouth

Use the shaker.

THIS WEEK'S BUY

Swedish Punch

16

TANGLEFOOT COCKTAIL
2 msr of fresh lemon juice   4 msr of Swedish punch
2 msr of fresh orange juice   4 msr of Bacardi rum

Use the shaker. Serve with a slice of orange.
Serves 4.

17

MELBA COCKTAIL
2 dashes of Pernod   2 dashes of grenadine
1^1/$_2$ msr of Swedish punch   1^1/$_2$ msr of Bacardi rum
The juice of half a lime or a quarter of a lemon

Use the shaker. Serve with a slice of lime and lemon and a cherry.

18

FAIR AND WARMER COCKTAIL
2 dash of blue Curaçao   1 msr of Italian vermouth
2 msr of Bacardi rum

Use the mixing glass. Serve with a cherry.

19

GREENBRIAR COCKTAIL
1 dash of peach bitters   2 msr of dry sherry
1 msr of French vermouth   1 sprig of fresh mint

Use the mixing glass.

YOUR OWN SPECIAL OCCASIONS AND COCKTAIL RATINGS

Swedish punch is a blend of rum, aquavit (schnapps), wine and syrup. Delicious served either hot or cold in cocktails.

Better than any prescription

From left: Waldorf Cocktail, Greenbriar Cocktail, Fair and Warmer Cocktail, Tanglefoot Cocktail, Melba Cocktail, Doctor Cocktail, Boomerang Cocktail.

May

20

BENTLEY COCKTAIL

1½ msr of Dubonnet   1½ msr of calvados

Use the shaker. Serve with a cherry.

Calvados is apple brandy made in the Normandy region of France.

21

TWELVE MILES OUT COCKTAIL

1 msr of Bacardi rum   1 msr of Swedish punch
1 msr of calvados

Use the mixing glass. Serve with a little lemon-peel juice squeezed on top and a slice of lemon.

THIS WEEK'S BUY

Calvados

22

STAR COCKTAIL

1 dash of French vermouth   1½ msr of calvados
1 dash of Italian vermouth   1½ msr of dry gin
1 tsp of fresh grapefruit juice

Use the shaker. Serve with slices of apple.

23

TIPPERARY COCKTAIL

3 dashes of grenadine   1 tsp of fresh orange juice
1 msr of Italian vermouth   2 msr of dry gin

Use the shaker. Serve with a sprig of mint.

24

ANGEL FACE COCKTAIL

1 msr of apricot brandy   1 msr of calvados
1 msr of dry gin

Use the shaker.

25

GINGER ALE CUP (non-alcoholic)

½ lb (225g) of loaf sugar   ½ teacupful of lime juice
2 pints (1.2 litres) of boiling water
1 bottle of ginger ale, preferably chilled

Dissolve sugar in the boiling water, chill. Place a large piece of ice in a glass jug or bowl, add ingredients, and stir well. Decorate with sprigs of fresh mint and fresh fruit. Serve immediately. Serves 4.

26

PRINCE'S SMILE COCKTAIL

1 dash of fresh lemon juice   1 tbsp of apricot brandy
1 tbsp of calvados   1½ msr of dry gin

Use the shaker. Serve with a slice of lemon.

YOUR OWN SPECIAL OCCASIONS AND COCKTAIL RATINGS

Clockwise from top left: Tipperary Cocktail, Bentley Cocktail, Star Cocktail, Prince's Smile Cocktail, Angel Face Cocktail, Ginger Ale Cup, Twelve Miles Out Cocktail.

May

27

RUM DAISY
1 tbsp of grenadine   3 msr of lemon juice
2 or 3 dashes brown or orange curaçao
3 msr of white rum

Shake well, and strain into an ice-filled tumbler. Top up with soda water. Stir and decorate with fruit. Alternative serving: strain into an ice-filled wine glass, omit soda water. Decorate with fruit. Half quantities for this method.

28

ROULETTE COCKTAIL
1 tbsp of Bacardi rum   1 tbsp of Swedish punch
1½ msr of calvados

Use the mixing glass.

29

NEW YORK COCKTAIL
1 lump of sugar   2 dashes of grenadine
1 piece of orange peel   3 msr Canadian Club whisky
The juice of a lime or half a lemon

Use the shaker. Serve with a little lemon-peel juice squeezed on top.

THIS WEEK'S BUY

Orange or Brown Curaçao

30

RYE FIZZ
5 or 6 dashes of grenadine   4½ msr of lemon juice
The white of an egg   3 msr Canadian Club whisky
1 tsp of brown or orange Curaçao

Use a shaker, strain into a highball glass, add ice. Top up with soda water if desired. Serve with straws.

31

CLARIDGE COCKTAIL
3 msr of apricot brandy   3 msr of Cointreau
1 msr of French vermouth   1 msr of dry gin

Use the shaker. Serve with a cherry.

June

1

WHISKY DAISY
1 msr of grenadine   3 msr of lemon juice
3 msr of lime juice   1½ msr of orange juice
3 msr of Scotch whisky

Shake and strain. Serve in an ice filled tumbler. Top up with soda water, stir and decorate. Alternative serving: strain half quantities into an ice-filled wine glass. Omit soda. Decorate with fruit.

2

WHITE COCKTAIL
2 dashes of orange bitters   3 msr of dry gin
6 dashes of anisette, or Pernod and a dash of sugar syrup

Use the mixing glass. Serve with lemon-peel juice squeezed on top.

The flavour may be improved by adding 2 dashes of brown Curaçao.

From left; Roulette Cocktail, Rye Fizz, New York Cocktail, Whisky Daisy, Claridge Cocktail, Rum Daisy, White Cocktail.

June

Cassis if a brandy-based
blackcurrant liqueur. It is a g*
way of making a cheap wine *
drinkable.

3

KIR COCKTAIL

1 glass of dry white wine,   1 tsp of crème de cassis
chilled

With a teaspoon, float crème de cassis on the wine.

4

CALVADOS COCKTAIL

4 msr of fresh orange juice   2 msr of Cointreau
2 msr of orange bitters   4 msr of calvados

Use the shaker. Serve with a slice of orange and apple.
Serves 4.

5

PARISIAN COCKTAIL

1 msr of French vermouth   1 msr of crème de cassis
1 msr of dry gin

Use the mixing glass. Serve in a frosted glass if desired. To
frost the glass: moisten the rim with crème de cassis, then
dip in caster sugar.

THIS WEEK'S BUY

Crème
de
Cassis/Port

6

DEMPSEY COCKTAIL

2 dashes of Pernod   3 dashes of grenadine
2 msr of calvados   1 msr of dry gin

Use the shaker. Serve with cherries.

7

PORT WINE SANGAREE

1 tsp of sugar   3 msr of water
6 msr of port

Dissolve sugar in water in a tumbler, add port and fill with
crushed ice. Stir well, decorate with grated nutmeg and
fruit if desired.

Ruby port is ideal for
cocktails, and keeps well.

8

ROOSEVELT COCKTAIL

1 msr of gin   1 msr of white rum
1 msr of lemon juice   1 msr of grenadine

Use the shaker.

9

PORT WINE COCKTAIL

1 dash of brandy   3 msr of port

Use the mixing glass. Serve with a little orange-peel juice
squeezed on top and a slice of orange.

YOUR OWN SPECIAL OCCASIONS AND COCKTAIL RATINGS

From left: Roosevelt Cocktail, Parisian Cocktail, Port Wine Cocktail, Kir Cocktail, Dempsey Cocktail, Calvados Cocktail, Port Wine Sangaree.

June

10
HAWAIIAN COCKTAIL
2 msr of dry gin   2 msr of orange juice
1 dash Cointreau

Shake.

11
MISSISSIPPI MULE COCKTAIL
2 msr of fresh lemon juice   2 msr of crème de cassis
8 msr of dry gin

Use the shaker. Serves 4.

12
GRAPEFRUIT COCKTAIL (1)
1 grapefruit   1 small tin of pineapple chunks
2 bananas   6 msr of sherry

Press grapefruit flesh through a sieve. Slice bananas and pineapple thinly and add to grapefruit puree. Sprinkle caster sugar on the fruit and pour the sherry over it. Stand on ice for an hour. Serve in sherbet glasses.

13
CASSIS HIGHBALL
1 msr of crème de cassis   1 msr of dry gin
Sparkling apple juice

Use the mixing glass for the gin and crème de cassis. Serve in a tumbler with a few lumps of ice and fill up with apple juice. Decorate with a slice of apple.

14
PINEAPPLE LEMONADE
1 small tin of pineapple chunks   2 lemons
¼ lb (100 g) of loaf sugar

Place lemon rind in a jug. Liquidise the pineapple and add with one pint (600 ml) of boiling water. Mix lemon juice with sugar and pour in. Strain. Add soda water and ice.

15
ICED TEA

Make the tea in the usual way, allowing one teaspoonful of tea to half a pint (600 ml) of water. Allow it to draw, then strain and leave to cool. Add a little sugar if desired, and some slices of lemon or fresh fruit juice: then stand on ice until required. Serve with small ice cubes.

16
GRAPE COCKTAIL
1 dash of Angostura bitters   1½ msr of grape juice
3 msr of sugar syrup   6 msr of soda water
Fresh fruit: grapes, oranges, lemons, strawberries

Use the mixing glass, half filled with broken ice. Add the bitters, grape juice and sugar syrup. Stir well, and strain into a tumbler. Fill with soda, and decorate with fruit.

A very refreshing drink as the da become warmer.

Take a fresh look at tea - some s it's the best drink in the world.

Clockwise from top left: Mississippi Mule Cocktail, Grape Cocktail, Pineapple Lemonade, Hawaiian Cocktail, Cassis Highball, Iced Tea, Grapefruit Cocktail (1).

June

17

PINK GIN COCKTAIL

1 dash of Angostura bitters   *3 msr of Plymouth gin*

Use the shaker.

Plymouth gin is unsweetened [and] the correct gin to use for a pink [gin,] the traditional gin of the Brit[ish] Royal Navy.

18

GIN FIX

2 tsp of sugar syrup   *The juice of half a lemon*
4½ msr of dry gin   *Water to taste*

Place ingredients in a tumbler, stir. Fill up glass with crushed ice. Decorate with fruit and serve with straws.

19

BIJOU COCKTAIL

1 dash of orange bitters   *1 msr of Plymouth gin*
1 msr of green Chartreuse   *1 msr of Italian vermouth*

Use the mixing glass. Serve with a cherry and a little lemon-peel juice squeezed on top.

THIS WEEK'S BUY

Plymouth Gin

20

'S.G.' COCKTAIL

3 dashes of grenadine   *1 msr of fresh lemon juice*
1 msr of fresh orange juice   *1 msr Canadian Club whisky*

Use the shaker.

21

CHAMPAGNE JULEP

1 lump of sugar   *2 sprigs of fresh mint*
Chilled champagne

Put sugar in a champagne glass, add sprigs of mint and gently crush leaves with a spoon. Fill with champagne. Stir gently. Decorate with seasonal fruit and mint.

Longest day and shortest nigh[t] the year (in the northern hemisphere). A good excuse to [crack] open the champagne!

22

OLIVETTE COCKTAIL

3 dashes of Pernod   *2 dashes of orange bitters*
2 dashes of sugar syrup   *3 msr of Plymouth gin*

Use the mixing glass. Serve with an olive and a little lemon-peel juice squeezed on top.

23

DEPTH CHARGE COCKTAIL

4 dashes of fresh lemon juice   *2 dashes of grenadine*
1½ msr of calvados   *1½ msr of brandy*

Use the shaker.

From left: 'S.G.' Cocktail, Bijou Cocktail, Gin Fix, Depth Charge Cocktail, Pink Gin Cocktail, Champagne Julep, Olivette Cocktail.

June

24
TEQUILA SUNRISE COCKTAIL
2 msr of tequila   4 msr of orange juice
A dash of grenadine

Shake well. Pour into the glass. Add dash of grenadine. Serve with straws.

25
BRANDY JULEP
1 tsp of caster sugar   4 tender sprigs of fresh mint
4$^1/_2$ msr of brandy

Cover mint with sugar in a tumbler. Add enough water to dissolve the sugar. Crush mint gently. Add brandy and fill glass with broken ice. Stir. Decorate with mint and fruit.

26
MARGARITA COCKTAIL
2 msr of tequila   2 msr of fresh lemon juice
1 msr of Cointreau

Shake. Frost rim of glass with salt.

27
STRAWBERRY CREAM COOLER
3 msr of gin   1$^1/_2$ msr of lemon juice
4$^1/_2$ msr of cream   3 strawberries
1 tsp of sugar

Blend for a few seconds. Pour into a tumbler and add soda water and ice cubes. Garnish with strawberries.

28
AMERICAN BEAUTY COCKTAIL
1 dash of crème de menthe   1 tbsp of French vermouth
1 tbsp of fresh orange juice   1 tbsp of brandy
1 tbsp of grenadine   A dash of port

Use the shaker. Serve with a little port wine on top, and a slice of orange.

29
STRAWBERRY DAWN
2 msr of gin   2 msr of coconut cream
3 fresh strawberries   2 scoops of crushed ice

Blend for a few seconds. Serve in a large glass.

30
BLOODHOUND COCKTAIL
3 crushed strawberries   1 tbsp of French vermouth
1 tbsp of Italian vermouth   1$^1/_2$ of dry gin

Use the shaker. Serve with a strawberry.

YOUR OWN SPECIAL OCCASIONS AND COCKTAIL RATINGS

Gold or silver (clear) tequila is a spirit distilled in Mexico.

Midsummer's Day.

From left: Strawberry Dawn, Bloodhound Cocktail, Tequila Sunrise, Margarita Cocktail, Strawberry Cream Cooler, American Beauty Cocktail, Brandy Julep Cocktail.

July

1
BANANA DAIQUIRI
3 msr of white rum   1½ msr of crème de banane
The juice of half a lime   Half a banana

Blend for a few seconds with two scoops of crushed ice.
Serve in a large wine glass.

2
CHERRY BLOSSOM COCKTAIL
1 dash of grenadine   1½ msr of cherry brandy
1 dash of orange Curaçao   1½ msr of brandy
1 dash of fresh lemon juice

Use the shaker. Serve very cold, with a fresh cherry.

3
BARRACUDA
3 msr of white rum   2 dashes of sugar syrup
1½ msr of Galliano   The juice of half a lime
3 msr of pineapple juice   Champagne

Use the shaker for all the ingredients *except* the champagne.
Serve in a pineapple shell and top with champagne.

4
BANANA BLISS
1½ msr of crème de banane   1 tbsp of orange juice
1½ msr of white rum   1 dash of Angostura bitters
1½ msr of cream   3-5 drops of grenadine

Use the shaker for all the ingredients except the grenadine.
Strain into a tumbler. Add the grenadine.

5
COMMODORE COCKTAIL
3 dashes of orange bitters   3 dashes of sugar syrup
The juice of half a lime or a quarter of a lemon
3 msr of Canadian Club whisky

Use the shaker. Serve with a slice of lemon and lime.

6
HOT DECK COCKTAIL
1 dash of Jamaica ginger   1 tbsp of Italian vermouth
3 msr of Canadian Club whisky

Use the mixing glass.

7
QUARTER DECK COCKTAIL
1 tsp of lime juice   1 msr of dry sherry
2 msr of rum

Use the mixing glass.

THIS WEEK'S BUY

Crème de Banane

YOUR OWN SPECIAL OCCASIONS AND COCKTAIL RATINGS

*Crème de banane is a sweet, cl
yellow banana flavour lique*

*You needn't be on the sea to en
these cocktails!*

 Clockwise from bottom left: Commodore Cocktail, Banana Daiquiri, Cherry Blossom Cocktail, Barracuda, Quarter Deck Cocktail, Banana Bliss, Hot Deck.

July

8

THIRD RAIL COCKTAIL
1 dash of Pernod   1 msr of calvados
1 msr of brandy   1 msr of bacardi rum

Use the shaker.

9

SHANDY GAFF
1/2 pint (300 ml) of ale, chilled
1/2 pint (300 ml) of ginger ale, chilled

Mix in a tumbler and serve ice cold, decorated with fruit.

THIS WEEK'S BUY

Applejack Brandy

10

APPLEJACK SOUR
2 dashes of sugar syrup   1 dash of grenadine
The juice of half a lemon (or equal parts of lemon and lime)
3 msr of applejack brandy or calvados

Mix in a shaker, half-filled with broken ice. Strain into a small wine glass. Add a little soda water, and decorate with apple.

11

APPLEJACK RABBIT COCKTAIL
2 msr of fresh lemon juice   4 msr of maple syrup
2 msr of fresh orange juice   4 msr of applejack brandy

Use the shaker. Serve with slices of orange and lemon and a cherry. Serves 4.

12

SUNDEW COCKTAIL
1 dash of Angostura bitters   1 1/2 msr of sugar syrup
1 1/2 msr of grape juice   3 msr of orange juice
2 slices of orange   4 1/2 msr of applejack brandy

Use the mixing glass. Stir well, and strain into a glass. Fill up with soda water, and decorate with fruit.

13

APPLEJACK HIGHBALL
4 1/2 msr of Applejack brandy   Soda water or ginger ale

Pour into a tumbler with a few lumps of ice. Serve with a piece of lemon peel or a slice of lemon.

14

JACK ROSE COCKTAIL
The juice of a lime or half a lemon
3 tbsp of applejack brandy or calvados
1 tbsp of grenadine

Use the shaker.

YOUR OWN SPECIAL OCCASIONS AND COCKTAIL RATINGS

Applejack brandy is produced in New England from the fermented mash of cider apples, then matured in wood for at least 2 years.

Clockwise from bottom left: Shandy Gaff, Applejack Highball, Applejack Rabbit Cocktail, Sundew Cocktail, Jack Rose Cocktail, Applejack Sour, Third Rail Cocktail (centre).

July

15

ICED CHOCOLATE
1 pint (600 ml) of chocolate   Vanilla ice cream

Make the chocolate in the normal way, and allow it to cool, then stand in a jug surrounded with ice or put in the refrigerator. When required, serve in small glasses topped with vanilla ice cream.

16

EGG LEMONADE (non-alcoholic)
The juice of a lemon   1 oz of caster sugar
1 egg

Prepare in the mixing glass, stir well, and strain into tumbler. Serve with water or soda water.

17

MIXED FRUIT COCKTAIL
Equal amounts of: Blackcurrants
Raspberries   Strawberries
Sugar to taste   A little lemon juice

Mash the fruits well, and add the sugar. Strain into the shaker, half filled with broken ice, and add the lemon juice and a little water. Shake, and strain into a wine glass.

18

CHERRY COCKTAIL
1 dash of Angostura bitters   2 dashes of lime juice
1½ msr of ginger syrup   1½ msr of cherry syrup
6 msr of soda water

Use the mixing glass, half filled with broken ice. Add all except the soda water, stir and strain into a tumbler. Fill up with soda water and decorate with fruit.

19

BLACKCURRANT COCKTAIL
2 tsp of powdered sugar   ¼ cupful of blackcurrrants
½ grapefruit

Cut a hole in the middle of the half-grapefruit, and fill with blackcurrants. Serve with powdered sugar.

20

RASPBERRY LEMONADE
1 lb (450 g) of raspberries   2 lemons
¼ lb (100 g) of caster sugar

Press the raspberries through a sieve, add the juice of the lemons and the sugar, stir well, and mix two pints (1.2 litres) of cold water. Serve with ice and decorate with raspberries.

21

ORANGEADE
4 oranges   2 lemons
2 lb (900 g) of loaf sugar

Scrape the rinds from the oranges and lemons by rubbing with the loaf sugar. Put the sugar in a jug, and pour 4 pints (2.25 litres) of boiling water over it. Add juice of the oranges and lemons, stir well, and cool. Strain and serve with fruit.

Very refreshing and contains lot vitamin C.

An attractive drink for all age

When raspberries go out of seas use some from the freezer.

YOUR OWN SPECIAL OCCASIONS AND COCKTAIL RATINGS

Clockwise from left: Iced Chocolate, Blackcurrant Cocktail, Egg Lemonade, Mixed Fruit Cocktail, Orangeade, Raspberry Lemonade, Cherry Cocktail.

67

22

ALLEN (Special) COCKTAIL
1 dash of lemon juice   1 msr of maraschino
2 msr of Plymouth gin

Use the shaker. Serve with a cherry.

23

CIDER CUP (2)
2 msr of Cointreau   1½ msr of maraschino
3 msr of brandy   4½ msr of dry sherry
1 tsp of lemon tea
2 pints (1.2 litres) of cider, preferably chilled

Place a large piece of ice in a glass jug or bowl. Add
ingredients, stir well, and decorate with fruit and sprigs of
fresh mint. (Serves 4.)

24

DEPTH BOMB COCKTAIL
1 dash of fresh lemon juice   4 dashes of grenadine
1½ msr of calvados   1½ msr of brandy

Use the shaker.

THIS WEEK'S BUY

Maraschino/ Yellow Chartreuse

25

RUM CRUSTA
1 tsp of sugar syrup   1 msr of lemon juice
2 dashes of Angostura bitters   1 tsp of maraschino
2 msr of white or dark rum

Use the shaker. Place a spiral of lemon rind in a frosted crusta
(small wine) glass, add ice and strained cocktail. Decorate with
seasonal fruit.

26

YELLOW PARROT COCKTAIL
1 msr of Pernod   1 msr of yellow Chartreuse
1 msr of apricot brandy

Use the shaker.

27

CHOCOLATE COCKTAIL (1)
1 tsp of powdered chocolate   The yolk of an egg
1½ msr of yellow Chartreuse   1½ msr of port

Use the shaker. Serve with a flake chocolate bar.

28

GOLDEN SLIPPER - a pousse café
The yolk of an egg   1 msr of yellow Chartreuse
1 msr of brandy

Add ingredients in the stated order, pour liquids over the
back of a spoon so that they touch the sides of the glass. Serve
in a pousse café glass. Do not stir, a layered effect should be
achieved.

YOUR OWN SPECIAL OCCASIONS AND COCKTAIL RATINGS

*Maraschino is an Italian liqueur
made with the sour black maraschino
cherries. The flavour is drier than
that of cherry brandy.*

*Don't let the name put you off
trying this one!*

*Yellow Chartreuse is sweeter and more
potent than the green variety. It is
made from over 130 types of herbs
and spices.*

Try this one after dinner.

Clockwise from left: Depth Bomb Cocktail, Allen (Special) Cocktail, Yellow Parrot Cocktail, Chocolate Cocktail (1), Golden Slipper, Rum Crusta, Cider Cup (2).

69

July

29

BRANDY CRUSTA
1 tsp of sugar syrup   *1 msr of lemon juice*
1 dash of Angostura bitters   *1 tsp of maraschino*
1 dash of orange bitters   *2 msr of brandy*

Use the shaker. Place a spiral of orange rind in a frosted crusta (small wine) glass, add ice and strained cocktail. Decorate with seasonal fruit.

30

TUXEDO COCKTAIL
1 dash of Pernod   *1 dash of maraschino*
2 dashes of orange bitters   *1½ msr of French vermouth*
1½ msr of dry gin

Use the mixing glass. Serve with grapes, slices of banana and a little lemon-peel juice squeezed on top.

31

SHERRY SANGAREE
1 tsp of sugar   *3 msr of water*
4½ msr of sherry

Dissolve sugar in the water in a tumbler, add sherry and fill with crushed ice. Stir well, decorate with grated nutmeg and cherries.

August

1

WHITE ROSE COCKTAIL
The juice of quarter of an orange
The juice of half a lime or a quarter of a lemon
The white of an egg   *1 tbsp of maraschino*
3 tbsp of dry gin

Use the shaker. Serve with seasonal fruit.

2

ICED COFFEE
12 msr strong coffee (made with freshly-ground coffee)
Sugar to sweeten   *12 msr vanilla-flavoured milk*
16 msr of cream   *Whipped cream*

Sweeten coffee while hot, then chill. Add milk and cream. Chill. Serve in glasses, topped with whipped cream.

3

CHOCOLATE COCKTAIL (2)
1 tsp of powdered chocolate   *1 egg*
1½ msr of yellow Chartreuse   *1½ msr of maraschino*

Use the shaker.

4

GRAPEFRUIT DRINK
1 grapefruit   *3 oranges*
¼ lb (100 g) of loaf sugar   *1 bottle soda water*

Rub the loaf sugar loaf on the rind of the oranges and then put it in a large jug. Pour over it one pint (600 ml) of water, the strained juice of the oranges and grapefruit. Strain, add a lump of ice and some soda water to serve.

A drink for any time of the d

Clockwise from left: Grapefruit Drink, White Rose Cocktail, Chocolate Cocktail, Sherry Sangaree, Tuxedo Cocktail, Iced Coffee, Brandy Crusta (centre).

5 — GREEN DRAGON COCKTAIL

8 dashes of peach bitters   1½ msr of fresh lemon juice
1½ msr of kummel   3 msr of crème de menthe
6 msr of dry gin

Use the shaker. Serves 4.

6 — HOCK CUP

1 bottle of hock, preferably chilled
1 pint (600 ml) of soda water, preferably chilled
1½ msr of kummel   3 msr of brandy
2 msr of yellow Chartreuse   1½ msr of maraschino

Place a large piece of ice in a glass jug. Add ingredients, stir well and decorate with fruit. Serve immediately. Serves 4.

7 — SILVER STREAK COCKTAIL

1½ msr of kummel   1½ msr of dry gin

Use the shaker.

8 — EGG PUNCH (non-alcoholic)

1 egg   1 tbs of vanilla syrup
Balance of milk & soda water   Ice

Beat the egg in a basin, and add vanilla syrup and chopped ice. Shake in the shaker, and strain into a long glass. Add the milk to three-quarters fill the glass, then fill up with soda water.

THIS WEEK'S BUY

Kummel

9 — DIPLOMAT COCKTAIL

1 dash of maraschino   2 msr of French vermouth
1 msr of Italian vermouth

Use the mixing glass. Serve with a cherry and a little lemon-peel squeezed on top.

10 — GIN CRUSTA

1 tsp of sugar syrup   1 msr of lemon juice
1 dash of Angostura bitters   1 dash of orange bitters
2 msr of gin   1 tsp of maraschino or pineapple syrup

Use the shaker. Place a spiral of orange rind in a frosted crusta (small wine) glass, add ice and strained cocktail.

11 — SUNSET COOLER

3 msr of Campari   6 msr of fresh orange juice

Pour into a tumbler, fill up with ice and stir. Decorate with a slice of orange.

Kummel comes mainly from Holland or Germany. This colourless liqueur is flavoured with many herbs and spices including caraway seeds.

The perfect drink when serving a crowd.

YOUR OWN SPECIAL OCCASIONS AND COCKTAIL RATINGS

 From left: Sunset Cooler, Gin Crusta, Diplomat Cocktail, Green Dragon Cocktail, Silver Streak Cocktail, Egg Punch, Hock Cup.

August

12

WESTERN ROSE COCKTAIL
1 dash of fresh lemon juice   1 tbsp of apricot brandy
1 tbsp of French vermouth   1½ msr of dry gin

Use the shaker.

13

INCA COCKTAIL
1 dash of orgeat syrup   1 dash of orange bitters
1 tbsp of dry gin   1 tbsp of dry sherry
1 tbsp of French vermouth   1 tbsp of Italian vermouth

Use the mixing glass. Decorate with a slice of orange.

14

PORTO FRAISE
3 msr of port   1 msr of fraisette (strawberry syrup)

Mix and serve in the same glass, add water or soda water and a lump of ice. Stir and serve.

15

SALTY DOG
3 msr of vodka   6 msr of grapefruit juice

Pour ingredients into an ice-filled, salt-frosted glass and stir. To frost the glass: moisten edges with lemon juice then dip into salt.

16

KIR ROYALE
2 dashes of crème de cassis   Chilled champagne

Serve in a champagne glass, stir carefully.

17

CLUB COCKTAIL
1 or 2 dashes of Angostura bitters
3 dashes of grenadine
3 msr of Canadian Club whisky

Use the mixing glass. Serve with a cherry and a little lemon-peel juice squeezed on top.

18

BRANDY COBBLER
1 tsp of sugar syrup   1 tsp of brown Curaçao
6 msr of brandy

Shake or mix well, and strain into a tumbler half-full of broken ice. Decorate slice of orange or lemon and a sprig of mint. Serve with a straw.

As an alternative to port use French vermouth.

A very special Kir.

YOUR OWN SPECIAL OCCASIONS AND COCKTAIL RATINGS

Clockwise from bottom left: Western Rose Cocktail, Inca Cocktail, Kir Royale, Brandy Cobbler, Salty Dog, Club Cocktail, Porto Fraise.

75

August

Amer Picon is a French aromatic wine with a slightly bitter flavour

19

BROOKLYN COCKTAIL
1 dash of Amer Picon   1 dash of maraschino
1 msr of French (or dry Martini) vermouth
2 msr of Canadian Club whisky

Use the mixing glass. Serve with a cherry.

20

WHISKY SOUR
1 tsp of sugar syrup   The juice of half a lemon
3 msr of Scotch whisky

Mix in a shaker, half-filled with broken ice. Strain into a small wine glass. If desired, add a little soda water, and decorate with a slice of lemon.

21

PICON COCKTAIL
1¹/₂ msr of Italian vermouth   1¹/₂ msr of Amer Picon

Use the mixing glass. Decorate with a slice of orange.

A good appetiser.

22

THIS WEEK'S BUY

Amer Picon

OPPENHEIM COCKTAIL
1 tbsp of grenadine   1 tbsp of Italian vermouth
1¹/₂ msr of Scotch whisky

Use the mixing glass.

23

PEGU CLUB COCKTAIL
1 dash of Angostura bitters   1 dash of orange bitters
3 dashes of lime juice   1 msr of Cointreau
2 msr of dry gin

Use the mixing glass. Serve with a piece of orange.

24

GRAPEFRUIT COCKTAIL (2)
¹/₂ grapefruit 1 orange Slices of banana The juice of a lemon
1 tbsp of sherry or white wine

Peel the grapefruit and orange, and break into sections. Arrange round side of a sherbet glass. Add slices of banana. Sprinkle with icing sugar, squeeze over the lemon juice and pour over the sherry or wine.

A dessert cocktail.

25

SILVER FIZZ
1 tsp of sugar syrup   The white of an egg
4¹/₂ msr of dry gin
The juice of a lemon, or equal parts of lemon and lime

Use a shaker, strain into a highball glass, add ice. Top with soda water, stir. Serve with straws and slices of lemon and/or lime.

From left: Whisky Sour, Brooklyn Cocktail, Pegu Club Cocktail, Oppenheim Cocktail, Silver Fizz, Picon Cocktail, Grapefruit Cocktail (2).

August

26
'OH, HENRY!' COCKTAIL
1 msr of ginger ale   1 msr of Bénédictine
1 msr of Scotch whisky

Use the mixing glass.

27
FIOUPE COCKTAIL
1 tsp of Bénédictine   1¹/₂ msr of Italian vermouth
1¹/₂ msr of brandy

Use the mixing glass. Serve with a cherry and a little lemon-peel juice squeezed on top.

28
CREOLE COCKTAIL
2 dashes of Amer Picon   2 dashes of Bénédictine
1¹/₂ of Italian vermouth   1¹/₂ msr Canadian Club whisky

Use the mixing glass. Serve with a little lemon-peel juice squeezed on top.

29
STRAITS SLING
The juice of half a lemon   2 dashes of Angostura bitters
2 dashes of orange bitters   1 tbsp of cherry brandy
1 tbsp of Bénédictine   3 msr of dry gin

Use the shaker. Strain into an ice-filled tumbler. Fill up with soda water, and stir. Serve with a cherry and slices of orange and lemon.

30
CARDINALE COCKTAIL
1¹/₂ msr of dry gin   1 tbsp of French vermouth (dry)
1 tbsp of Campari

Shake and strain into a cocktail glass.

31
ORIENTAL COCKTAIL
The juice of half a lime   1 tbsp of Cointreau
1 tbsp of Italian vermouth   1¹/₂ msr Canadian Club whisky

Use the shaker.

September

1
WHISKY RICKEY
The juice of half a lime   4¹/₂ msr of Scotch whisky

Mix in a tumbler with a lump of ice. Fill up with soda water, and stir well. Serve with a slice of lime.

YOUR OWN SPECIAL OCCASIONS AND COCKTAIL RATINGS

Bénédictine could be one of the oldest liqueurs in the world. It originated in Fécamp, Normandy where it was produced by the Bénédictine monks.

From left: Straits Sling, Cardinale Cocktail, Whisky Rickey, Oriental Cocktail, Creole Cocktail, Fioupe Cocktail, 'Oh Henry!' Cocktail.

September

2
SLOE GIN COCKTAIL
1 tbsp of French vermouth   1 tbsp of Italian vermouth
1¹/₂ msr of sloe gin

Use the mixing glass.

Sloe gin is a sweet red liqueur, made by soaking sloe berries in gin.

3
APPLEJACK RICKEY
The juice of half a lime   4¹/₂ msr of applejack brandy

Mix in a tumbler with a lump of ice. Fill up with soda water, and stir well.

THIS WEEK'S BUY

Sloe Gin

4
BLACKTHORN COCKTAIL
2 dashes of orange bitters   1 msr of Italian vermouth
1 msr of French vermouth   1 msr of sloe gin

Use the mixing glass. Serve with a cherry and a little lemon-peel juice squeezed on top.

Sloe berries are the fruit of the blackthorne shrub - try making some sloe gin this autumn - though the best sloe gin is matured for 10 years!

5
PLANTER'S COCKTAIL
1 tbsp of sugar syrup   1¹/₂ msr of white rum
1 tbsp of fresh lime juice (or lemon juice)

Use the mixing glass. Serve with a slice of lime.

6
OPENING COCKTAIL
1 tbsp of grenadine   1 tbsp of Italian vermouth
1¹/₂ msr of Canadian Club whisky

Use the mixing glass.

A perfect beginning to an evening.

7
BURGUNDY CUP
3 msr of brandy   3 msr of maraschino
2 or 3 dashes of Bénédictine   1¹/₂ msr of brown Curaçao
1 bottle of burgundy, preferably chilled
1 bottle of soda water, preferably chilled

Place a large piece of ice in a glass jug or bowl. Add ingredients, stir well, decorate with fruit. Serves 4.

Only wine and soda to purchase - other ingredients have been accumulated over the previous months.

8
ONE EXCITING NIGHT COCKTAIL
1 dash of orange juice   1 msr of French vermouth
1 msr of Italian vermouth   1 msr of Plymouth gin

Use the shaker. Serve with a little lemon-peel juice squeezed on top.

YOUR OWN SPECIAL OCCASIONS AND COCKTAIL RATINGS

 From top left: Planter's Cocktail, Blackthorn Cocktail, One Exciting Night Cocktail, Applejack Rickey, Burgundy Cup, Opening Cocktail, Sloe Gin Cocktail.

September

9

KING COLE COCKTAIL

1 dash of Fernet Branca   2 dashes of sugar syrup
3 msr of Scotch whisky

Use the mixing glass. Decorate with slices of orange and pineapple.

10

PORT COBBLER

5 dashes of sugar syrup   1 or 2 dashes of brandy
4¹/₂ msr of port

Mix well, and strain into a tumbler half-full of broken ice. Decorate with fruit, and serve with a straw.

11

BLUE COOLER

The juice of half a lime   3 msr of white rum
1¹/₂ msr of blue Curaçao   6 msr of pineapple juice

Stir ingredients in a tumbler. Add ice. Serve with straws.

THIS WEEK'S BUY

Fernet
Branca

12

BERMUDIAN ROSE COCKTAIL

2 msr of dry gin   1 msr of apricot brandy
1 msr of grenadine   1 msr of lemon juice

Use the shaker. Decorate with a slice of fresh apricot, if available, and a cherry.

13

BRANDY FLIP

The yolk of an egg   3 msr of brandy
Sugar or sugar syrup to taste

Prepare in the shaker, half-filled with broken ice. Shake well, and strain into a wineglass: serve with grated nutmeg on top.

14

MILLIONAIRE COCKTAIL (2)

1 dash of grenadine   The juice of a lime
1 msr of apricot brandy   1 msr of rum
1 msr of sloe gin

Use the shaker. Decorate with a cherry.

15

SLOE GIN RICKEY

The juice of half a lime   4¹/₂ msr of sloe gin

Mix in a tumbler with a lump of ice. Fill up with soda water, stir well, and serve with a slice of lime.

YOUR OWN SPECIAL OCCASIONS AND COCKTAIL RATINGS

Fernet Branca is an Italian herbal-flavoured bitters. It is dr[unk] as a digestive after meals, and famous in the UK as a hango[ur] remedy.

A delicious drink - and what [a] colour!

From left: Brandy Flip, Sloe Gin Rickey, King Cole Cocktail, Millionaire Cocktail, Port Cobbler, Blue Cooler, Bermudian Rose Cocktail.

September 16

RUSTY NAIL COCKTAIL
1 msr of Drambuie   2 msr of Scotch whisky

Serve in the old-fashioned (whisky/rocks) glass on ice.

17

STARS AND STRIPES - a pousse café
Equal parts of: Crème de cassis
Maraschino   Green Chartreuse

Serve in a pousse café glass, adding ingredients in the stated order to form a layered effect. Pour liqueurs over the back of a spoon, held so that it touches the sides of the glass.

18

JERSEY LILY - a pousse café
Equal parts of: Yellow Chartreuse
Old brandy

Serve as above.

THIS WEEK'S BUY

Drambuie

19

AFTER DINNER COCKTAIL (1)
1$\frac{1}{2}$ of apricot brandy   1$\frac{1}{2}$ msr of Cointreau
The juice and grated rind of a lime

Use the shaker. Serve with a slice of orange.

20

HOT SCOTCH
The juice of a lemon   2 lumps of sugar
3 msr of Scotch whisky

Put ingredients in a glass, fill up with boiling water, stir well.

21

AFTER SUPPER COCKTAIL
1$\frac{1}{2}$ msr of Cointreau   1$\frac{1}{2}$ msr of apricot brandy
4 dashes of fresh lemon juice

Use the shaker.

22

BOBBY BURN'S COCKTAIL
3 dashes of Bénédictine   1$\frac{1}{2}$ msr of Italian vermouth
1$\frac{1}{2}$ msr of Scotch whisky

Use the mixing glass. Serve with a little lemon-peel juice squeezed on top and a cherry.

YOUR OWN SPECIAL OCCASIONS AND COCKTAIL RATINGS

Drambuie is the oldest of the whisky liqueurs, the main ingredients being heather, honey and whisky.

A steady hand is a necessary ingredient here.

Any brandy will float in just the same way.

Clockwise from top left: After Supper Cocktail, Bobby Burns Cocktail, After Dinner Cocktail, Stars and Stripes, Jersey Lily, Hot Scotch, Rusty Nail Cocktail.

September 23

IRISH COFFEE

Hot coffee   *2 tsp of sugar*
2 msr of Irish whiskey   *Fresh double cream*

Pour coffee into a glass, stir in sugar and whiskey. Pour cream over the back of a warmed spoon, very gently. Do not stir.

24

PADDY COCKTAIL

1 dash of Angostura bitters   *1¹/₂ msr of Italian vermouth*
1¹/₂ msr of Irish whiskey

Use the mixing glass.

25

SOUTHERN GIN COCKTAIL

2 dashes of orange bitters   *2 dashes of Cointreau*
3 msr of dry gin

Use the shaker. Serve with a little lemon-peel juice squeezed on top.

26

SHAMROCK COCKTAIL

3 dashes of green Chartreuse   *1¹/₂ msr of French vermouth*
3 dashes of green crème de menthe
1¹/₂ msr of Irish whiskey

Use the mixing glass.

THIS WEEK'S BUY

Irish Whiskey

27

DRAMBUIE SWIZZLE

3 msr of Drambuie   *1¹/₂ msr of lime cordial*
1 drop of orange bitters   *Soda water*

Half fill a tumbler with ice, add Drambuie, lime cordial and bitters. Top up with soda water, stir. Decorate with a sprig of mint, or a slice of lime.

28

JOHNNIE MACK COCKTAIL

3 dashes of Pernod   *1 msr of orange Curaçao*
2 msr of sloe gin

Use the mixing glass. Serve with a little lemon-peel juice squeezed on top.

29

PRAIRIE OYSTER COCKTAIL

The yolk of an egg   *2 dashes of vinegar*
1 tsp of Worcester sauce   *1 tsp of tomato ketchup*

Mix all the ingredients except the egg-yolk. Then drop the egg-yolk in the glass without breaking it. Serve with a dash of pepper on the top.

A real pick-me-up!

Clockwise from top: Johnnie Mack Cocktail, Paddy Cocktail, Shamrock Cocktail, Drambuie Swizzle, Prairie Oyster, Irish Coffee, Southern Gin Cocktail (centre).

September 30

RUM FIX
1 tsp of sugar syrup	The juice of half a lemon
1½ msr dark or white rum	1½ msr of cherry brandy

A little water to taste

Place ingredients in a tumbler, stir. Fill up glass with crushed ice. Decorate with fruit and serve with straws.

October 1

SENSATION COCKTAIL
3 dashes of maraschino	3 sprigs of fresh mint
1 tbsp of fresh lemon juice	3 tbsp of dry gin

Use the shaker. Serve with a cherry and fresh mint, if available.

2

BITTER COCKTAIL
The juice of a lemon	The juice of half an orange

3 dashes of Angostura bitters

Use the shaker, half-filled with broken ice, and strain into a wine glass. A little sugar or sugar syrup may be added, according to taste.

You could try this at breakfast time.

3

THIS WEEK'S BUY

Dark and Golden Rum

RASPBERRY COOLER
1½ msr of raspberry syrup	1½ msr of dry gin
1 tbsp of lime juice	2 dashes of grenadine
1 dash of maraschino	⅓ pint of ginger ale

Place ingredients in a mixing glass. Stir. Pour into a tumbler half-filled with ice.

4

WEST INDIAN COCKTAIL
4 dashes of Angostura bitters	3 dashes of fresh lemon juice
3 dashes of sugar syrup	1 lump of ice

3 msr of dry gin

Stir and serve in the same glass.

5

JAMAICAN COFFEE
Hot coffee	2 tsp of sugar
2 msr of dark rum	Fresh double cream

Pour coffee into a glass, stir in sugar and rum. Pour cream over back of warmed spoon, very gently. DO NOT STIR.

An after-dinner treat.

6

BLUE HAWAIIAN
1½ msr of white rum	1 tbsp of blue Curaçao
3 msr of pineapple juice	1½ msr of coconut cream

Blend with a scoop of crushed ice for a few seconds, and serve in a champagne flute with a cherry and a slice of pineapple.

YOUR OWN SPECIAL OCCASIONS AND COCKTAIL RATINGS

 Clockwise from left: Sensation Cocktail, Rum Fix, Blue Hawaiian, West Indian Cocktail, Raspberry Cooler, Jamaican Coffee, Bitter Cocktail.

October

7 — GIN COBBLER
1 tsp of sugar syrup   1 tsp of blue Curaçao
6 msr of gin

Shake or mix well, and strain into a tumbler half-full of broken ice. Decorate with fruit and serve with a straw.

8 — WHISKY SMASH
½ lump of sugar   4 sprigs of fresh mint
3 msr of Scotch whisky

Dissolve sugar in water, stir in mint briefly and remove. Half fill shaker with ice, add whisky, shake and strain. Stir, decorate with fruit and small straws.

9 — MILK PUNCH
3 msr of brandy   1½ msr of dark rum
1 tbsp of sugar syrup   Balance of milk

This may be prepared cold (in the shaker, half-filled with broken ice) or hot (by heating the milk). Serve with grated nutmeg on top.

THIS WEEK'S BUY

Kahlua

10 — ATTA BOY COCKTAIL
4 dashes of grenadine   1 msr of French vermouth
2 msr of dry gin

Use the shaker. Serve with a little lemon-peel juice squeezed on top.

11 — BLACK RUSSIAN COCKTAIL
1 msr of vodka   1 msr of kahlua

Stir and serve on ice.

12 — BRAVE BULL COCKTAIL
1 msr of tequila   1 msr of kahlua

Over ice. Use old-fashioned (whisky/rocks) glass.

13 — DRAMBUIE SHRUB
1½ msr of Drambuie   4½ msr of chilled orange juice
1 scoop of lemon water ice

In a goblet mix the Drambuie and orange juice. Top with water ice. Serve with straws and a small spoon. Decorate with a sprig of mint.

Kahlua originates from Mexico; it is a coffee liqueur.

YOUR OWN SPECIAL OCCASIONS AND COCKTAIL RATINGS

From left: Milk Punch, Gin Cobbler, Black Russia Cocktail, Drambuie Shrub, Whisky Smash, Brave Bull Cocktail, Atta Boy Cocktail.

14

PICON GRENADINE
3 msr of Amer Picon   1 msr of grenadine

Mix and serve this aperitif in the same glass, add water or
soda water and a lump of ice. Stir and serve.

15

BLENTON COCKTAIL
1 dash of Angostura bitters   2 msr of Plymouth gin
1 msr of French (or dry Martini) vermouth

Use the shaker. Serve with a cherry and a little lemon-peel
juice squeezed and then served on top.

16

APRICOT LADY
1½ msr of golden rum   1½ msr of apricot brandy
1 tbsp of fresh lime juice   3 dashes of orange Curaçao
2 dashes of egg white

Blend with a small scoop of crushed ice for a few seconds.
Serve in a large wine glass with a slice of orange.

17

DAIQUIRI COCKTAIL
2 msr of white rum   2 tsp of sugar
1 tbsp of fresh lime or lemon juice

Use the shaker.

18

APPLE PIE COCKTAIL
2 dashes of apricot brandy   1½ msr of bacardi rum
1½ msr of Italian vermouth

Use the shaker.

19

KNICKERBOCKER COCKTAIL
1 dash of Italian vermouth   1 msr of French vermouth
2 msr of dry gin

Use the mixing glass. Serve with a little lemon-peel juice
squeezed on top.

20

WHISKY FIX
2 tsp of sugar syrup   The juice of half a lemon
4½ msr of Scotch whisky   Water to taste

Place ingredients in a tumbler, stir. Fill up glass with crushed
ice. Decorate with fruit and serve with straws.

YOUR OWN SPECIAL OCCASIONS AND COCKTAIL RATINGS

From left: Picon Grenadine, Blenton Cocktail, Daiquiri Cocktail, Apricot Lady, Knickerbocker Cocktail, Apple Pie Cocktail, Whisky Fix.

21

ADONIS COCKTAIL

1 dash of orange bitters   2 msr of dry sherry
1 msr of Italian vermouth

Use the mixing glass. Serve with a piece of orange.

22

ALICE MINE COCKTAIL

2 dashes of Scotch whisky   1½ msr of Italian vermouth
1½ msr of kummel

Use the mixing glass. Serve with a cherry.

23

BLUE BOAR

3 tbsp of vodka   1 tbsp of Drambuie
1 tbsp of blue Curaçao   1 dash of lemon squash
The white of an egg

Use the shaker. Serve with a fresh flower.

THIS WEEK'S BUY

Grand Marnier

24

ARTIST'S SPECIAL COCKTAIL

2 msr of fresh lemon juice
2 msr of gooseberry syrup   4 msr of dry sherry
4 msr of Scotch whisky

Use the mixing glass. Serve with a slice of lemon.
Serves 4.

25

YELLOW DAISY COCKTAIL

1 dash of Pernod   1 msr of French vermouth
1 tbsp of Grand Marnier   1 msr of dry gin

Use the shaker. Serve with a cherry.

26

TROCADERO COCKTAIL

1 dash of orange bitters   1 dash of grenadine
1½ msr of French vermouth   1½ msr of Italian vermouth

Use the mixing glass. Serve with a cherry and a little
lemon-peel juice squeezed on top.

27

ALLIES COCKTAIL

2 dashes of kummel   1½ msr of French vermouth
1½ msr of dry gin

Use the shaker.

YOUR OWN SPECIAL OCCASIONS AND COCKTAIL RATINGS

From left: Artist's Special Cocktail, Allies Cocktail, Yellow Daisy Cocktail, Trocadero Cocktail, Blue Boar Cocktail, Alice Mine Cocktail, Adonis Cocktail.

28 BRANDY PUNCH

The juice of half a lemon   *1 tbsp of sugar syrup*
2 or 3 dashes of Cointreau   *4½ msr of brandy*

Prepare in a shaker, half-filled with broken ice. Strain into an ice-filled tumbler. Decorate with seasonal fruits.

29 PORT WINE FLIP

The yolk of an egg   *3 msr of port*
Sugar syrup to taste

Prepare in a shaker, half-filled with broken ice. Shake well, and strain into a wine glass. Serve with grated nutmeg on top.

30 MACARONI COCKTAIL

1 msr of Italian vermouth   *2 msr of Pernod*

Use the mixing glass.

THIS WEEK'S BUY

Amaretto
di
Saronno

31 SATAN'S WHISKERS COCKTAIL

1 dash of orange bitters   *1 tbsp of fresh orange juice*
1 tbsp of French vermouth   *1 tbsp of Italian vermouth*
1 tbsp of Grand Marnier   *1 tbsp of dry gin*

Use the shaker. Serve with a slice of orange.

1 AMARETTO SOUR

1½ msr of fresh lemon juice   *3 msr of Amaretto do Saronno*

Make in a shaker, half-filled with broken ice. Strain into a frosted tulip champagne glass. Decorate with a slice of orange. To frost the glass: moisten edges with lemon juice then dip in caster sugar.

2 BLUSHING BARMAID

1½ msr of Amaretto di Saronno   *1½ msr of Campari*
The white of half an egg   *3 msr of bitter lemon*

Shake Amaretto, Campari and egg white with broken ice. Strain into an ice-filled glass. Top up with bitter lemon, stir. Decorate with lemon, fresh apricot and a cherry.

3 ORANGE BLOOM COCKTAIL

1 tbsp of Cointreau   *1 tbsp of Italian vermouth*
1½ msr of dry gin

Use the shaker. Serve with a cherry.

4 QUIET SUNDAY

3 msr of vodka   *1½ msr of Amaretto di Saronno*
6 msr of fresh orange juice   *1 dash of grenadine*

Mix vodka, Amaretto di Saronno and orange juice in a shaker, half-filled with ice. Strain into an ice-filled tumbler, then add a dash of grenadine.

YOUR OWN SPECIAL OCCASIONS AND COCKTAIL RATINGS

Hallowe'en.

This delicious almond-flavour Italian liqueur was first made in Saronno in the sixteenth century.

A super drink any day of the week.

Mischief Night! - autumn's equivalent to April Fool's Day.

Clockwise from top: Amaretto Sour, Quiet Sunday Cocktail, Orange Bloom Cocktail, Brandy Punch, Macaroni Cocktail, Blushing Barmaid Cocktail, Port Wine Flip, Satan's Whiskers Cocktail (centre).

November

5

OXFORD PUNCH

3 parts of dark rum   2 parts of brandy
1 part of lemon squash   6 parts of boiling water
Sugar to taste

This can serve any number of persons, provided that the proportions of the ingredients are kept the same.
Stir all together in a punch bowl.

6

BLACKCURRANT TEA (non-alcoholic)

1 tbsp of blackcurrant jelly   4 lumps of sugar
1 dessertspoonful of lemon juice

Mix together in a jug, and add a tumblerful of boiling water.
Stir well, and stand the jug in a pan of boiling water for 20 minutes. Then strain and serve.

7

DRAMBUIE COFFEE

Hot coffee   2 tsp of sugar
2 msr of Drambuie   Fresh double cream

Pour coffee into a glass, stir in sugar and Drambuie. Pour cream over the back of a warmed spoon, very gently.
DO NOT STIR.

8

GLÜHWEIN

12 msr of red wine   2 lumps of sugar
1 slice of lemon   1 slice of orange
A pinch of cinnamon

Heat all ingredients.

9

HOT TEA PUNCH

3 pints of freshly brewed tea   1 pint of brandy
1 bottle dark rum   Sugar to taste

Mix well, and mull with a red-hot poker. Decorate with orange and lemon peel. Serves at least 12.

10

PORT WINE EGG NOGG

1 egg   1 tsp of sugar syrup
4 1/2 msr of port   1 1/2 msr of brandy
1 1/2 msr of rum   6 msr of milk

Prepare in a shaker, half-filled with broken ice. Strain, sprinkle with grated nutmeg. Stir in more milk if desired.

11

SCOTCH MILK PUNCH

4 1/2 msr of Scotch whisky   3 dashes of lemon juice
1 tbsp of sugar syrup   Balance of milk

This may be prepared cold (in a shaker, half-filled with broken ice) or hot (by heating the milk). Serve with grated nutmeg on top.

Guy Fawkes Night. A warming drink after the bonfire has died down.

Perfect for the children - or those with a sweet tooth.

A lovely warming drink, a favourite in ski resorts.

Clockwise from left: Hot Tea Punch, Port Wine Egg Nog, Scotch Milk Punch, Drambuie Coffee, Gluhwein, Blackcurrant Tea, Oxford Punch.

November 12

STINGER COCKTAIL
1 tbsp of white crème de menthe   3 tbsp of brandy

Use the shaker. Serve very cold.

Try this cocktail after dinner as crème de menthe has very good digestive properties.

13

LORD SUFFOLK COCKTAIL
1½ msr of maraschino
1½ msr of Cointreau   1½ msr of Italian vermouth
7½ msr of dry gin

Use the shaker. Serve with a little lemon-peel juice squeezed on top. Serves 4.

14

BRANDY COLLINS
1 tsp of sugar syrup   4½ msr of brandy
The juice of one lemon or 2 limes

Make in a shaker, half-filled with broken ice. Strain into a tumbler, add ice and fill up with soda water. Stir. Decorate with fruit. Serve with straws.

THIS WEEK'S BUY

White Crème de Menthe

15

PALL MALL COCKTAIL
1 dash of orange bitters   1 tsp of white crème de menthe
1 msr of French vermouth   1 msr of Italian vermouth
1 msr of dry gin

Use the mixing glass.

This liqueur has exactly the same flavour as the better known green crème de menthe. No colour has been added.

16

BRANDY HIGHBALL
4½ msr of brandy   Ginger ale or soda

Serve in a tumbler with a few lumps of ice. Serve with a piece of lemon peel or a slice of lemon.

17

GOLDEN CADILLAC COCKTAIL
1 msr of Galliano   1 msr of cream
1 msr of white Curaçao or Cointreau

Use the shaker.

18

MARTINI COCKTAIL (medium)
1 tbsp of Italian vermouth   1½ msr of dry gin
1 tbsp of French (or dry Martini) vermouth

Use the mixing glass. Serve with a little lemon-peel juice squeezed and then served on top.

YOUR OWN SPECIAL OCCASIONS AND COCKTAIL RATINGS

 Clockwise from top left: Golden Cadillac Cocktail, Brandy Collins, Brandy Highball, Stinger Cocktail, Martini Cocktail, Lord Suffolk Cocktail, Pall Mall Cocktail.

November **19**

NAPOLEON COCKTAIL

1 dash of orange Curaçao   1 dash of Fernet Branca
1 dash of Dubonnet   3 msr of dry gin

Use the mixing glass. Serve with a cherry and a little lemon-peel juice squeezed on top.

20

WHISKY COLLINS

1 tsp of sugar syrup   4¹/₂ msr of Scotch whisky
The juice of one lemon or two limes

Use the shaker, half-filled with broken ice. Strain into a tumbler, add ice and fill up with soda water. Stir. Decorate with fruit. Serve with straws.

21

EMMAGREEN

1¹/₂ msr of dry gin   1 tbsp of fresh orange juice
1 tbsp of Amaretto di Saronno   1 tbsp of blue Curaçao
The white of half an egg
3 msr well-chilled sparkling wine or champagne

Half-fill a shaker with broken ice. Shake all ingredients and strain into frosted tumbler. Top up with champagne.

> **THIS WEEK'S BUY**
>
> Lillet

22

'HOOP-LA!' COCKTAIL

1 tbsp of fresh lemon juice   1 tbsp of Lillet
1 tbsp of Cointreau   1 tbsp of brandy

Use the shaker. Serve with a slice of orange.

23

DUBONNET CITRON

3 msr of Dubonnet   1 msr of sirop de citron

Mix and serve this apéritif in the same glass. Add water or soda water and a lump of ice. Stir and serve. As alternatives to Dubonnet use Amer Picon, Lillet or Campari.

24

BAMBOO OR REFORM COCKTAIL

1 dash of orange bitters   1¹/₂ msr of dry sherry
1¹/₂ msr of French vermouth

Use the mixing glass. Serve with a little lemon-peel juice squeezed on top.

25

'HOOTS MON' COCKTAIL

1 tbsp of Lillet   1 tbsp of Italian vermouth
1¹/₂ msr of Scotch whisky

Use the mixing glass.

YOUR OWN SPECIAL OCCASIONS AND COCKTAIL RATINGS

A really colourful experience

Lillet is a vermouth-type drink.

Clockwise from top left: Napoleon Cocktail, Whisky Collins, Emmagreen, Hoop-la Cocktail, Bamboo Cocktail, Hoots-Mon Cocktail, Dubonnet Citron.

WINTER SUNRISE
1½ msr of Campari   1½ msr of dry gin
6 msr of pineapple juice

Pour into a tumbler, fill up with ice, stir. Decorate with fruit.

27

RUM COLLINS
1 tsp of sugar syrup   4½ msr of rum (white or dark)
The juice of one lemon or two limes

Make in a shaker, half-filled with broken ice. Strain into a tumbler, add ice and fill up with soda water. Stir. Decorate with fruit. Serve with straws.

28

ALASKA COCKTAIL
2 dashes of orange bitters   1 tbsp of yellow Chartreuse
3 tbsp of dry gin

Use the shaker. Serve with a little lemon-peel juice squeezed on top.

29

ALEXANDER COCKTAIL (1)
1 msr of crème de cacao   1 msr of sweetened cream
1 msr of brandy

Use the shaker. Decorate with some grated chocolate.

THIS WEEK'S BUY

Crème de Cacao

30

OLD-FASHIONED COCKTAIL
1 lump of sugar   2 dashes of Angostura bitters
4½ msr Canadian Club whisky   The peel of half a lemon

Prepare and serve in a tumbler. Put the sugar in first, then add the Angostura bitters, and muddle. Add the whisky and a cube of ice, and stir. Squeeze lemon-peel juice on top.

December 1

ALEXANDER COCKTAIL (2)
1 tbsp of crème de cacao   1 tbsp of sweetened cream
1½ msr of dry gin

Use the shaker. Decorate with a chocolate flake.

2

MARTINEZ COCKTAIL
1 dash of orange bitters   2 dashes of maraschino
1½ msr of French vermouth   1½ msr of dry gin

Use the mixing glass. Serve with an olive and a little lemon-peel juice squeezed on top.

YOUR OWN SPECIAL OCCASIONS AND COCKTAIL RATINGS

Crème de cacao is a sweeet cocoa/vanilla flavoured liqueur. It comes from Cacao, a part of Venezuela.

St Andrew's Day. (Patron saint of Scotland.)

Try the Alexander cocktails after dinner.

From left: Alexander Cocktail (2), Martinez Cocktail, Rum Collins, Old-Fashioned Cocktail, Winter Sunrise, Alexander Cocktail (1), Alaska Cocktail.

3

SPANISH TOWN COCKTAIL

2 or 3 dashes of Cointreau   3 msr of white rum

Use the shaker.

4

BLUE CRUSTA

2 msr of blue Curaçao   1 msr of lemon juice
1 dash of Angostura bitters   1 tsp of brandy

Make in a shaker half-filled with broken ice. Place a spiral of lemon rind in a frosted crusta (small wine) glass. Add ice and strained cocktail. Decorate with fruit.

5

SPECIAL POUSSE CAFÉ

1 tsp of grenadine   1 msr of green crème de menthe
1 tsp of Galliano   1 msr of kummel
1 msr of brandy

Serve in a pousse café glass, add ingredients in stated order to form a layered effect. Pour liquids over the back of a spoon.

6

CALYPSO COFFEE

Hot coffee   2 tsp of sugar
1 msr of Tia Maria   1 msr of light rum
Fresh double cream

Pour coffee into a wine glass, stir in sugar, Tia Maria and light rum. Pour cream over the back of a warmed spoon, very gently. DO NOT STIR.

7

ANGEL'S TIP COCKTAIL

2 msr of crème de cacao   1 tbsp of fresh cream

Float cream on top. Decorate with a little grated chocolate.

8

GRASSHOPPER COCKTAIL

1 msr of green crème de menthe   1 msr of white crème de cacao
1 msr of fresh cream

Shake and serve in champagne glass with straws.

9

NEWTON'S SPECIAL COCKTAIL

1 dash of Angostura bitters   1 tbsp of Cointreau
3 tbsp of brandy

Use the mixing glass.

THIS WEEK'S BUY

Tia Maria

YOUR OWN SPECIAL OCCASIONS AND COCKTAIL RATINGS

Tia Maria is a Jamaican coffee flavoured liqueur.

From left: Blue Crusta, Angel's Tip Cocktail, Grasshopper Cocktail, Newton's Special Cocktail, Special Pousse Café, Calypso Coffee, Spanish Town Cocktail.

107

10

CROW COCKTAIL
1 dash of grenadine   2 msr of fresh lemon juice
1 msr of Scotch whisky

Use the mixing glass.

11

RUM HIGHBALL
4½ msr of white or dark rum   Lemonade or soda water

Serve in a tumbler with a few lumps of ice. Serve with a piece of lime peel or a slice of lime.

12

MARY PICKFORD COCKTAIL
3 dashes of grenadine   6 drops of marachino
1½ msr of fresh pineapple juice   1½ msr of Bacardi rum

Use the mixing glass.

THIS WEEK'S BUY

Kirsch

13

RAFFLES KNOCKOUT COCKTAIL
2 msr of Kirsch   2 msr of Cointreau
1 dash of fresh lemon

Shake, and serve in champagne glass. Add cherries.

14

HOT FRUIT DRINK
Fruit syrup   The juice of a lemon
Sugar to taste

Dilute one part of fruit syrup with two parts of hot water, add the sugar and lemon juice, and serve.

15

K.C.B. COCKTAIL
1 dash of apricot brandy   1 dash of fresh lemon juice
1 tbsp of Kirsch   3 tbsp of dry gin

Use the shaker. Serve with a little lemon-peel juice squeezed on top.

16

GIN HIGHBALL
4½ msr of dry gin   2 dashes of Angostura bitters
Soda water

Serve in a tumbler with a few lumps of ice, a piece of lemon peel or a slice of lemon.

YOUR OWN SPECIAL OCCASIONS AND COCKTAIL RATINGS

Kirsch is a colourless brandy made from wild cherries and their stones.

From left: Crow Cocktail, K.C.B. Cocktail, Gin Highball, Rum Highball,
Raffles Knockout Cocktail, Mary Pickford Cocktail, Hot Fruit Drink.

December 17

PORT WINE NEGUS

1 wine-glassful of port wine   1 lemon
Sugar to taste

Put the wine in a long glass, and add the sugar and the rind and juice of the lemon. Fill up with boiling water, and strain.

A great drink for unexpected guests - perhaps carol singers

18

THREE MILLER COCKTAIL

3 dashes of grenadine   1 dash of fresh lemon juice
1 msr of Bacardi rum   2 msr of brandy

Use the shaker.

19

HEART STIRRER

1½ msr of Amaretto di Saronno
Chilled Veuve du Vernay or dry sparkling white wine

Pour Amaretto di Saronno into a champagne glass, top up with wine, stir carefully.

A very special drink.

20

VERMOUTH CASSIS HIGHBALL

4½ msr of French vermouth   1 tsp of crème de cassis
Soda water or lemonade

Serve in a tumbler with a few lumps of ice, and cherry, and a piece of lemon peel or a slice of lemon.

21

BUCK'S FIZZ COCKTAIL

The juice of an orange   Top with champagne

Use large goblet or champagne glass.

A classic cocktail - a lovely party drink.

22

ORIENT EXPRESS

1 msr of Drambuie   1 msr of French vermouth
1 msr of Canadian Club whisky

Use the mixing glass. Stir ingredients in equal proportions over ice. Strain into a cocktail glass. Serve with a piece of orange peel.

23

AFTER DINNER BLUES

1½ msr of blue Curaçao   1 tbsp of fresh double cream

Float the cream on the Curaçao. DO NOT STIR.

Clockwise from top left: Port Wine Negus, Heart Stirrer, Buck's Fizz Cocktail, Vermouth Cassis Highball, After Dinner Blues, Orient Express Cocktail, Three Miller Cocktail.

December

24

GRAND SLAM COCKTAIL

1 tbsp of French vermouth   1 tbsp of Italian vermouth
1¹/₂ msr of Swedish punch

Use the mixing glass. Serve with a slice of lemon.

25

MONTE CARLO IMPERIAL COCKTAIL

1 tbsp of fresh lemon juice   1 tbsp of crème de menthe
1¹/₂ msr of dry gin

Use the shaker. Strain into a wine-glass, and fill up with champagne.

A festive drink for Christmas Day.

26

WHISKY SANGAREE

1 tsp of sugar   3 msr of water
4¹/₂ msr of Scotch whisky

Dissolve sugar in the water in a whisky tumbler. Add whisky and fill with crushed ice. Stir well, decorate with grated nutmeg. Serve with straws.

27

NORMANDY COFFEE

Hot coffee   2 tsp of sugar
2 msr of Bénédictine   Fresh double cream

Pour coffee into a glass, stir in sugar and Bénédictine. Pour cream over the back of a warmed spoon, very gently. DO NOT STIR.

28

HOT BUTTERED RUM

2 tbsp of dark rum   2 tsp of sugar
2 tsp of butter
¹/₂ tsp of mixed spices (cinnamon and cloves)

Put the ingredients in a tumbler, fill up with boiling water, and stir well.

29

GRENADIER COCKTAIL

3 dashes of grenadine   1¹/₂ msr of ginger wine
1¹/₂ msr of brandy

Use the shaker. Serve with a strawberry or a slice of orange.

30

PRAIRIE HEN COCKTAIL

2 dashes of vinegar   1 tsp of Worcester sauce
1 egg   2 dashes of Tabasco sauce
Pepper and salt

Mix all the ingredients except the egg. Then drop the egg in the glass without breaking it.

A real pick-me-up between Christmas and New Year Festivities.

31

ZOMBIE

1¹/₂ msr of white rum   1¹/₂ msr of dark rum
1¹/₂ msr of apricot brandy   1 tbsp of orange juice
1 tbsp of lemon juice   1 tbsp of pineapple juice
A little 151% proof demararan rum

Use shaker for all the ingredients except the Demararan rum. Strain and pour into a highball glass half-filled with crushed ice. Pour over the demararan rum. Garnish with fruit.

A fitting end to the year. This is the most lethal cocktail of them all.

YOUR OWN SPECIAL OCCASIONS AND COCKTAIL RATINGS

Clockwise from bottom left: Hot Buttered Rum, Prairie Hen, Grand Slam Cocktail, Monte Carlo Imperial Cocktail, Grenadier Cocktail, Normandy Coffee, Whisky Sangaree, Zombie Cocktail (centre).

Ingredients guide

If you have just one or two bottles in your drinks cabinet, this guide will help you to find the cocktails you can make using them. Since most cocktails are based on gin, brandy, rum, vermouth, Scotch whisky, Canadian Club whisky or vodka the cocktails are listed under those headings. To find, for example, a cocktail containing gin and rum, look under the main heading Gin-based Cocktails and then under the sub-heading Gin/rum. The two cocktails you will find listed here do not also appear under Rum-based Cocktails, avoiding repetition. Mixers and non-alcoholic extras (see page 8 for the list of these) are not included in the ingredients guide.

Gin-based Cocktails

Gin only
Belmont Cocktail
Bennett Cocktail
Bulldog Cooler
Café de Paris Cocktail
Clover Club Cocktail
Cream Fizz
Gimlet Cocktail
Gin Daisy
Gin Fix
Gin Highball
Gin Sling
Grapevine Cocktail
Hot Gin
Orange Blossom Cocktail (1)
Orange Blossom Cocktail (2)
Orange Fizz
Pink Lady Cocktail
Pink Rose Cocktail
Raspberry Cooler
Royal Fizz
Silver Fizz
Strawberry Cream Cooler
Strawberry Dawn
West Indian Cocktail
White Cocktail
Whiz-bang Cooler

Gin/rum
Bacardi Special Cocktail
Roosevelt Cocktail

Gin/vermouth
Atta Boy Cocktail
Bloodhound Cocktail
Cooperstown Cocktail
Knickerbocker Cocktail
Martini Cocktail (dry)
Martini Cocktail (medium)
Martini Cocktail (sweet)
Polo Cocktail
Queen's Cocktail
R.A.C. Cocktail
Velocity Cocktail
Yellow Rattler Cocktail

Gin/vermouth/ apricot brandy
Western Rose Cocktail

Gin/vermouth/calvados
Star Cocktail

Gin/vermouth/Campari
Cardinale Cocktail
Negroni Cocktail

Gin/vermouth/Cointreau
Journalist Cocktail
Luigi Cocktail
Orange Bloom Cocktail

Gin/vermouth/créme de cassis
Parisian Cocktail

Gin/vermouth/Dubonnet
Café Royal Appetiser Cocktail
Dubonnet Cocktail
Royal Cocktail

Gin/vermouth/Grand Marnier
Satan's Whiskers Cocktail

Gin/vermouth/green Charteuse
Sandmartin Cocktail

Gin/vermouth/kummel
Allies Cocktail

Gin/vermouth/maraschino
Martinez Cocktail

Gin/vermouth/sherry
Inca Cocktail

Gin/apricot brandy
Bermudian Rose Cocktail
Fairy Belle Cocktail
Paradise Cocktail

Gin/apricot brandy/calvados
Angel Face Cocktail
Prince's Smile Cocktail

Gin/blue Curaçao
Blue bird Cocktail
Gin Cobbler

Gin/Campari
Tropical Dawn
Winter Sunrise

Gin/cherry brandy
Singapore Sling

Gin/cherry brandy/Bénédictine
Straits Sling

Gin/Cointreau
Hula-hula Cocktail
Hawaiian Cocktail
Pegu Club Cocktail
Southern Gin Cocktail

Gin/crème de cassis
Cassis Highball

Gin/crème de menthe
Alexander's Sister Cocktail
Fallen Angel Cocktail
Monte Carlo Imperial Cocktail

Gin/crème de menthe/kummel
Green Dragon Cocktail

Gin/kummel
Silver Streak Cocktail

Gin/maraschino
Gin Crusta
Sensation Cocktail
White Rose Cocktail

Gin/Pernod
Café de Paris Cocktail
London Cocktail
Monkey Gland Cocktail

Gin/Pernod/calvados
Dempsey Cocktail

Gin/sherry
Roc-a-coe Cocktail

Gin/Swedish punch
Waldorf Cocktail

Brandy-based Cocktails

Brandy only
Brandy Collins
Brandy Daisy
Brandy Flip
Brandy Highball
Brandy Julep
Brandy Smash
Brandy Sour
Cider Cup (1)
Grenadier Cocktail
Plain Egg Nogg

Brandy/white rum
Hot Tea Punch
Oxford Punch
Scorpion
Three Miller Cocktail

Brandy/white rum/port
Port Wine Egg Nogg

Brandy/vermouth
Charles Cocktail
Washington Cocktail

Brandy/vermouth/Bénédictine
Fioupe Cocktail

Brandy/vermouth/Pernod
Presto Cocktail

Brandy/apricot brandy
Cuban Cocktail

Brandy/blue Curaçao
Blue Crusta
Bosom Caresser Cocktail
Breakfast Egg Nogg
East India Cocktail

Brandy/calvados
Depth Bomb Cocktail
Depth Charge Cocktail

Brandy/cherry brandy
Brandy Fix
Vanderbilt Cocktail

Brandy/cherry brandy/orange Curaçao
Cherry Blossom Cocktail

Brandy/Cointreau
Brandy Punch
Claret Cup
Egg Sour
Newton's Special Cocktail
Rolls-Royce Cocktail
Sidecar Cocktail

Brandy/crème de menthe
Emerald Cooler

Brandy/green Chartreuse
Champs Elysées Cocktail

Brandy/maraschino
Brandy Crusta

Brandy/orange Curaçao
Brandy Cobbler

Brandy/port
Port Cobbler
Port Wine Cocktail

Brandy/yellow Chartreuse
Golden Slipper
Jersey Lily

Brandy/yellow Chartreuse/Pernod
Yellow Parrot Cocktail

Rum-based Cocktails

White rum only
Bacardi cocktail
Casablanca
Cuba Libre
Daiquiri Cocktail
Piña Colada
Plain Egg Nogg
Planter's Cocktail
Rum Collins
Rum Cooler
Rum Highball

Rum/vermouth/apricot brandy
Apple Pie Cocktail

Rum/vermouth/blue Curaçao
Fair and Warmer Cocktail

Rum/apricot brandy/sloe gin
Millionaire Cocktail (2)

Rum/blue Curaçao
Blue Cooler
Blue Hawaiian

Rum/brown or orange Curaçao
Rum Daisy

Rum/cherry brandy
Rum Fix

Rum/Cointreau
Spanish Town Cocktail
Spring Shake-up

Rum/crème de banane
Banana Bliss
Banana Daiquiri

Rum/ Galliano
Barracuda

Rum/maraschino
Mary Pickford Cocktail
Rum Crusta

Rum/Pernod
Bacardi Crusta

Rum/sherry
Quarterdeck Cocktail

Rum/swedish punch
Melba Cocktail
Tanglefoot Cocktail

Rum/swedish punchCalvados
Roulette Cocktail
Twelve Miles Out Cocktail

Vermouth-based Cocktails

Vermouth only
Addington Cocktail
Club Cooler
Raymond Hitch Cocktail
Trocadero Cocktail
Wyoming Swing Cocktail

Vermouth/ Scotch whisky
Affinity Cocktail
Oppenheim Cocktail
Rob Roy Cocktail
Thistle Cocktail
Wembley Cocktail

Vermouth/ Scotch whisky/Bénédictine
Bobby Burns Cocktail

Vermouth/Scotch whisky/cherry brandy
Blood and Sand Cocktail

Vermouth/Scotch whisky/Kummel
Alice Mine Cocktail

Vermouth/Canadian Club whisky
Hot Deck Cocktail
Los Angeles Cocktail
Manhattan Cocktail (dry)
Mountain Cocktail

Vermouth/Canadian Club whisky/Amer Picon
Creole Cocktail

Vermouth/ Canadian Club whisky/Campari
Old Pal Cocktail

Vermouth/Canadian Club whisky/Cointreau
Oriental Cocktail

Vermouth/Canadian Club whisky/Drambuie
Orient Express

Vermouth/Canadian Club whisky/Dubonnet
Soul's Kiss Cocktail

Vermouth/Canadian Club whisky/ Swedish punch
Boomerang Cocktail

Vermouth/vodka
Vodkatini Cocktail

Vermouth/Amer Picon
Picon Cocktail

Vermouth/crème de cassis
Crème de Cassis Highball

Vermouth/green Chartreuse/Plymouth gin
Bijou Cocktail

Vermouth/Irish whiskey
Paddy Cocktail

Vermouth/Irish whiskey/crème de menthe
Shamrock Cocktail

Vermouth/maraschino
Diplomat Cocktail

Vermouth/sherry
Bamboo or Reform Cocktail
Greenbriar Cocktail

Vermouth/sloe gin
Blackthorn Cocktail
Sloe Gin Cocktail

Vermouth/swedish punch
Grand Slam Cocktail

Scotch whisky-based Cocktails

Scotch whisky only
Crow Cocktail
Gaelic Coffee
Hot Scotch
Scotch Milk Punch
Scotch Mist Cocktail
Whisky Collins
Whisky Cooler
Whisky Daisy
Whisky Fix
Whisky Rickey
Whisky Sangaree
Whisky Smash
Whisky Sour
Whisky Toddy

Scotch whisky/Bénédictine
'Oh Henry!' Cocktail

Scotch whisky/Fernet Branca
King Cole Cocktail

Scotch whisky/Pernod
Linstead Cocktail
Morning Glory Fizz
White Horse Daisy

Scotch whisky/sherry
Artist's Special Cocktail

Canadian Club whisky-based Cocktails

Candian Club whisky only
Club Cocktail
Commodore Cocktail
Ink Street Cocktail
New York Cocktail
New York Cooler
Old-Fashioned Cocktail
Rock and Rye Cocktail
'S.G.' Cocktail

Canadian Club whisky/blue Curaçao
Millionaire Cocktail (1)

Canadian Club whisky/brown or orange Curaçao
Rye Fizz

Canadian Club whisky/ Cointreau/Dubonnet
Dandy Cocktail

Canadian Club whisky/Pernod
Ladies' Cocktail

Vodka-based Cocktails

Vodka only
Bloody Mary
Harvey Wallbanger
Salty Dog
Screwdriver Cocktail

Vodka/blue Curaçao/ Drambuie
Blue Boar

Vodka/Campari
S.W.1. Cocktail

Vodka/Cointreau
Balalaika Cocktail

Vodka/Kahlua
Black Russian Cocktail

Types of cocktail

Party Cocktails
Brandy Punch
Buck's Fizz Cocktail
Champagne Cobbler
Champagne Julep
Cider Cup (1 and 2)
Claret Cup
Glühwein
Hock Cup
Hot Tea Punch
Moselle Cobbler
Valentine's Champagne Cocktail

Long and Cool Drinks
Angostura Fizz
Applejack Highball
Apricot Lady
Banana Bliss
Banana Daiquiri
Blue Cooler
Brandy Cobbler
Brandy Collins
Brandy Daisy
Brandy Fix
Brandy Highball
Brandy Julep
Brandy Smash
Bulldog Cooler
Casablanca
Cassis Highball
Club Cooler
Cream Fizz
Cuba Libre Cocktail
Drambuie Swizzle
Emerald Cooler
Gin Cobbler
Gin Daisy
Gin Highball
Gin Sling
Ginger Ale Cup
Grape Cocktail
Morning Glory Fizz
New York Cooler
Orange Fizz
Piña Colada
Port Cobbler
Port Wine Sangaree
Raspberry Cooler
Royal Fizz
Rum Collins
Rum Cooler
Rum Daisy
Rum Fix

Rum Highball
Rye Fix
Scorpion
Shandy Gaff
Sherry Sangaree
Silver Fizz
Singapore Sling
Sloe Gin Rickey
Spring Shake-up
Straits Sling
Strawberry Cream Cooler
Strawberry Dawn
Sundew Cocktail
Sunset Cooler
True Blue
Vermouth Cassis Highball
Whisky Collins
Whisky Cooler
Whisky Daisy
Whisky Rickey
Whisky Sangaree
Whisky Smash
White Horse Daisy
Whiz-bang Cooler
Wyoming Swing

Non-alcoholic Cocktails
Blackcurrant Cocktail
Blackcurrant Tea
Bitter Cocktail
Cherry Cocktail
Egg Lemonade
Egg Punch
Ginger Ale Cup
Grapefruit Drink
Grapefruit and Orangeade
Hot Fruit Drink
Ice Chocolate
Iced Coffee
Iced Tea
Mixed Fruit Cocktail
Pineapple Lemonade
Pussy Foot Cocktail
Orangeade
Raspberry Lemonade
Sundew Cocktail

Breakfast Cocktails
Bitter Cocktail
Breakfast Egg Nogg

Special Occasion Cocktails
Alfonso Cocktail
Barracuda Cocktail
Black Velvet Cocktail
Blue Hawaiian
Buck's Fizz Cocktail
Champagne Cobbler

Champagne Julep
Emmagreen
Golden Dream Cocktail
Heart Stirrer
Kir Royale
Monte Carlo Imperial Cocktail
Valentine's Champagne Cocktail

Coffees
Calypso Coffee
Drambuie Coffee
Gaelic Coffee
Iced Coffee
Irish Coffee
Jamaican Coffee
Normandy Coffee

After Dinner Cocktails
After Dinner Blues
After Dinner Cocktail
After Supper Cocktail
Alexander Cocktail (1 and 2)
Alexander's Sister Cocktail
Angel's Tip Cocktail
Bobby Burns Cocktail
Chocolate Cocktail (1 and 2)
Golden Slipper
Grasshopper Cocktail
Grenadier Cocktail
Jersey Lily
Newton's Special Cocktail
Port Wine Cocktail
Raffles Knockout Cocktail
Rusty Nail Cocktail
Spanish Town Council
Special Pousse Café
Stars and Stripes

Dessert Cocktails
Grapefruit Cocktail (1 and 2)
Drambuie Shrub

Night Caps
Ale Posset
Hot Buttered Rum
Hot Gin
Hot Scotch
Milk Punch
Plain Egg Nogg
Port Wine Egg Nogg
Port Wine Flip
Port Wine Negus
Scotch Milk Punch
Whisky Toddy

Pick-me-ups
Prairie Hen Cocktail
Prairie Oyster Cocktail

Index

(in alphabetical order)